The Natural History of Chocolate

Being a Distinct and Particular Account of the Cocoa-Tree, its Growth and Culture, and the Preparation, Excellent Properties, and Medicinal Vertues of its Fruit

D. de Quelus

Contents

PREFACE 7
PART I. 9
   CHAP. I. The Description of the *Cocao-Tree*. 9
   CHAP. II. Of the Choice and Disposition of the Place for Planting *Cocao-Trees*. 14
   CHAP. III. Of the Method of Planting a Nursery,..
      and to cultivate it till the Fruit comes to Maturity. 18
   CHAP IV. Of the gathering of the *Cocao-Nuts*, and the Manner of ....
      making them sweat, and of drying them that they may be brought sound into *Europe* 23

THE Natural HISTORY OF CHOCOLATE. 31
PART II. Of the Properties of Chocolate. 31
   CHAP. I. Of the old Prejudices against Chocolate. 31
   CHAP. II. Of the real Properties of Chocolate. 35
      SECT. I. Chocolate is very Temperate. 35
      SECT. II. Chocolate is very nourishing and of easy Digestion. 36
      SECT. III. Chocolate speedily repair the dissipated Spirits and decay'd Strength. 38
      SECT. IV. Chocolate is very proper to preserve Health, and to prolong the Life of Old Men 40

THE Natural HISTORY OF *CHOCOLATE*. 44
PART III. Of the Uses of Chocolate. 44
   CHAP. I Of Chocolate in Confections. 44
   CHAP. II. Of Chocolate, properly so called. 45
   SECT. I Of the Original of Chocolate, and the different Manners of preparing it. 45
      The Method of making Chocolate after the ....
      Manner of the *French* Islands in *America*. 48
   SECT. II. Of the Uses that may be made of Chocolate with relation to Medicine. 49
   CHAP. III. Of the Oil or Butter of Chocolate. 52

MEDICINES In whose Composition OIL or BUTTER OF *CHOCOLATE* Is made use of. 59

THE NATURAL HISTORY OF CHOCOLATE

BEING A DISTINCT AND PARTICULAR ACCOUNT OF

THE COCOA-TREE, ITS GROWTH AND CULTURE, AND

THE PREPARATION, EXCELLENT PROPERTIES,

AND MEDICINAL VERTUES OF ITS FRUIT

BY

D. de Quelus

The SECOND EDITION.
LONDON:
Printed for J. ROBERTS,
near the *Oxford-Arms* in *Warwick-Lane*. M DCC.XXX.

PREFACE

If the Merit of a Natural History depends upon the Truth of the Facts which are brought to support it, then an unprejudiced Eye-Witness is more proper to write it, than any other Person; and I dare even flatter myself, that this will not be disagreeable to the Publick notwithstanding its Resemblance to the particular Treatises of **Colmenero**[1], **Dufour**[2], and several others who have wrote upon the same Subject. Upon examination, so great a Difference will appear, that no one can justly accuse me of having borrow'd any thing from these Writers.

This small Treatise is nothing but the Substance and Result of the Observations that I made in the **American Islands**, during the fifteen Years which I was obliged to stay there, upon the account of his Majesty's Service. The great Trade they drive there in **Chocolate**, excited my Curiosity to examine more strictly than ordinary into its Origin, Culture, Properties, and Uses. I was not a little surprized when I every day discover'd, as to the Nature of the Plant, and the Customs of the Country, a great Number of Facts contrary to the Ideas, and Prejudices, for which the Writers on this Subject have given room.

For this reason, I resolved to examine every thing myself, and to represent nothing but as it really was in Nature, to advance nothing but what I had experienced, and even to doubt of the Experiments themselves, till I had repeated them with the utmost Exactness. Without these Precautions, there can be no great Dependance on the greatest Part of the Facts, which are produced by those who write upon any Historical Matter from Memorandums; which, from the Nature of the

---

1 De Chocolata Inda.
2 Du The, du Caffe, & du Chocolat.

Subject, they cannot fully comprehend.

As for my Reasonings upon the Nature, Vertues, and Uses of Chocolate, perhaps they may be suspected by some People, because they relate to an Art which I do not profess; but let that be as it will, the Facts upon which they are founded are certain, and every one is at liberty to make what other Inferences they like best.

As there are several Names of Plants, and Terms of Art used in those Countries, which I have been obliged to make use of, and which it was necessary to explain somewhat at large, that they might be rightly understood; rather than make frequent Digressions, and interrupt the Discourse, I have thought fit to number these Terms, and to explain them at the End of this Treatise: the Reader must therefore look forward for those Remarks under their particular Numbers.

PART I.
CHAP. I.
The Description of the *Cocao-Tree*.

The *Cocao-Tree* is moderately tall and thick, and either thrives, or not, according to the Quality of the Soil wherein it grows: Upon the Coast of *Caraqua*, for instance, it grows considerably larger than in the Islands belonging to the *French*.

Its **Wood** is porous, and very light; the **Bark** is pretty firm, and of the Colour of *Cinnamon*, more or less dark, according to the Age of the Tree. The **Leaves** are about nine Inches long, and four in breadth, where they are broadest; for they grow less towards the two Extremities, where they terminate in a point: their Colour is a little darkish, but more bright above than underneath; they are joined to Stalks three Inches long, and the tenth part of an Inch broad. This Stalk, as it enters the Leaf, makes a strait Rib, a little raised along the Middle, which grows proportionably less the nearer it comes to the End. From each side of this Rib proceed thirteen or fourteen crooked Threads alternately.

As these Leaves only fall off successively, and in proportion as others grow again, this Tree never appears naked: It is always flourishing, but more especially so towards the two **Solstices**, than in the other Seasons.

The **Blossoms**, which are regular and like a Rose, but very small, and without smell, proceed from the Places from which the old Leaves fall, as it were in Bunches. A large Quantity of these fall off, for hardly Ten of a Thousand come to good, insomuch that the Earth underneath seems cover'd over with them.

Every **Blossom** is joined to the Tree by a slender Stalk half an Inch or a little more in length; when it is yet in the Bud, it is one Fifth of an Inch broad, and about one fourth or a little more in length: when it was least, in proportion to the Tree and the Fruit, the more strange it appeared to me, and more worthy of Attention[a].

When the Buds begin to blow, one may consider the *Calix*, the *Foliage*, and the Heart of the Blossom. The *Calix* is formed of the Cover of the Bud, divided into five Parts, or Leaves, of a very pale flesh-colour. These are succeeded by the five true Leaves of the same Colour, which fill up the empty Spaces or Partitions of the *Calix*. These Leaves have two Parts, the undermost of which is like an oblong Cup, striped with Purple; on the inside, it bends towards the Center by the help of a *Stamen*, which serves to fasten it; from this proceeds outwardly, the other Part of the Leaf, which seems to be separate from it, and is formed like the End of a Pike.

The Heart is composed of five Threads and five *Stamina*, with the *Pistilla* in the middle. The Threads are strait, and of a purple Colour, and placed over-against the Intervals of the Leaves. The *Stamina* are white, and bend outwardly with a kind of a Button on the top, which insinuates itself into the middle of each Leaf to sustain itself.

When one looks at these small Objects through a Microscope, one is ready to say, That the Point of the Threads is like Silver, and that the *Stamina* are Chrystal; as well as the *Pistilla*, which Nature seems to have placed in the Center, either to be the *Primitiae* of the young Fruit, or to serve to defend it, if it be true that this Embryo unfolds itself, and is produced in no other place but the Base.

For want of observing these small Parts, as well as the Bulk of the Blossom, *F. Plumier* had no distinct Knowledge of them, nor has he exactly design'd them, any more than *Mons. Tournefort*, who has done them after his Draught[b].

The *Cocao-Tree* almost all the Year bears Fruit of all Ages, which ripen successively, but never grow on the end of little Branches, as our Fruits in *Europe* do, but along the Trunk and the chief Boughs, which is not rare in these Countries, where several Trees do the like; such as the [1] *Cocoeiers*, the [2] *Apricots* of St. *Domingo*, the [3] *Calebashes*, the [4] *Papaws*, &c.

Such an unusual Appearance would seem strange in the Eyes of *Europeans*, who had never seen any thing of that kind; but if one examines the Matter a little, the philosophical Reason of this Disposition is very obvious. One may easily apprehend, that if Nature had placed such bulky Fruit at the Ends of the Branches, their great Weight must necessarily break them, and the Fruit would fall before it came to Maturity.

The Fruit of the *Cocao-Tree* is contained in a Husk or Shell, which from an exceeding small Beginning, attains, in the space of four Months, to the Bigness and Shape of a Cucumber; the lower End is sharp and furrow'd length-ways like a Melon[c].

This Shell in the first Months is either red or white, or a Mixture of red and yellow: This Variety of Colours makes three sorts of *Cocao-Trees*, which have nothing else to distinguish them but this, which I do not think sufficient to make in reality three different kinds of *Cocao-Nuts* [d].

The First is of a dark vinous Red, chiefly on the sides, which becomes more bright and pale as the Fruit ripens.

The Second, which is the White, or rather is at first of so pale a Green, that it may be mistaken for White; by little and little it assumes a Citron Colour, which still growing deeper and deeper, at length becomes entirely yellow.

The Third, which is Red and Yellow mix'd together, unites the Properties of the other two; for as they grow ripe, the Red becomes pale, and the Yellow grows more deep.

I have observed that the white Shells are thicker and shorter than the other, especially on the side towards the Tree, and that these sorts of Trees commonly bear most.

If one cleaves one of these Shells length-ways, it will appear almost half an Inch thick, and its Capacity full of Chocolate Kernels; the Intervals of which, before they are ripe, are fill'd with a hard white Substance, which at length turns into a Mucilage of a very grateful Acidity: For this reason, it is common for People to take some of the Kernels with their Covers, and hold them in their Mouths, which is mighty refreshing, and proper to quench Thirst. But they take heed of biting them, because the Films of the Kernels are extreamly bitter.

When one nicely examines the inward Structure of these Shells, and anatomizes, as it were, all their Parts; one shall find that the Fibres of the Stalk of the Fruit passing through the Shell, are divided into five Branches; that each of these Branches is subdivided into several Filaments, every one of which terminates at the larger End of these Kernels, and all together resemble a Bunch of Grapes, containing from twenty to thirty-five single ones, or more, ranged and placed in an admirable Order.

I cannot help observing here, what Inconsistency there is in the Accounts concerning the Number of Kernels in each Shell. [e] ***Dampier***, for instance, says there is commonly near a Hundred; other Moderns[f] 60, 70 or 80, ranged like the Seeds of a Pomgranate. [g] ***Thomas Gage***, 30 or 40; ***Colmenero*** [h] 10 or 12; and ***Oexmelin*** [i] 10 or 12, to 14.

I can affirm, after a thousand Tryals, that I never found more nor less than twenty-five. Perhaps if one was to seek out the largest Shells in the most fruitful Soil, and growing on the most flourishing Trees, one might find forty Kernels; but as it is not likely one should ever meet with more, so, on the other hand, it is not probable one should ever find less than fifteen, except they are abortive, or the Fruit of a Tree worn out with Age in a barren Soil, or without Culture.

When one takes off the Film that covers one of the Kernels, the Substance of it appears; which is tender, smooth, and inclining to a violet Colour, and is seemingly divided into several Lobes, tho' in reality they are but two; but very irregular, and difficult to be disengaged from each other, which we shall explain more clearly in speaking of its Vegetation. [k] ***Oexmelin*** and several others have imagined, that a ***Cocao***-Kernel was composed of five or six Parts sticking fast together; Father ***Plumier*** himself fell into this Error, and has led others into it[l]. If the Kernel be cut in two length-ways, one finds at the Extremity of the great end, a kind of a longish [m]Grain, one fifth of an Inch long, and one fourth Part as broad, which is the ***Germ***, or first Rudiments of the Plant; but in ***European*** Kernels this Part is placed at the other end.

One may even see in ***France*** this Irregularity of the Lobes, and also the ***Germ*** in the Kernels that are roasted and cleaned to make Chocolate.

NOTES:

[a] ***Piso*** says (***Montiss. Aromat. cap. 18.***) that the Blossom is great and of a bright Yellow, ***Flos est magnus & flavescens instar Croci***. A modern Author has transcribed this. Error of ***Piso***; ***Floribus***, says he, ***mag-***

nis pentapetalis & flavis. **Dale** Pharmacologia, ***Pag. 441***.

[b] Appen. Rei Herbariae. ***pag.*** 660. ***tab.*** 444.

[1] [2] [3] [4] See the Remarks at the End of this Treatise.

[c] **Benzo** says they grow ripe in a Year, as well as others after him, ***Annuo Spatio maturescit, Benzo memorante***. Carol. Cluzio, l. c. ***Annuo justam attingens Maturitatem Spatio***. Franc. Hernandes, ***apud*** Anton. Rech. ***In Hist. Ind. Occidental***, lib. 5. c. 1.

[d] It seems likely that the **Spanish** Authors who say there are four Kinds of this at **Mexico**, have no better Foundation for the difference than this; and Mons. **Tournefort** had reason to say after Father **Plumier**, that he only knew one Kind of this Tree. Cacao **Speciem Unicam novi**. ***Append. Rei Herb.*** pag. 660.

[e] ***A new Voyage round the World.*** Tom. 1. Ch. 3. p. 69.

[f] Pomet's ***General History of Drugs***, Book vii. Ch. xiv. pag. 205. Chomel's ***Abridgment of usual Plants***. Valentin. Hist. Simplicium reform. lib. 2.

[g] New Relation of the ***East Indies***. Tom. 1. Part 2. Ch. 19.

[h] A curious Discourse upon Chocolate, by **Ant. Colmenero de Cedesma**, Physician and Chirurgeon at **Paris** 1643.

[i] ***The History of Adventures.*** Tom. 1. Pag. 423.

[k] Ibid.

[l] In multas veluti Amygdalas fissiles. **Tournefort** in Append. Rei Herb. ***Pag. 660. & Tab. 444.***

[m] I can't imagine upon what Foundation **Oexmelin** could assert, that the **Spaniards** in the making of their Chocolate, used nothing but this longish Grain, which he calls ***Pignon***. Au Milieu desquelles Amandes de Cacao, est, ***says he***, un petit Pignon, qui a la Germe fort tendre, & difficile a conserver; c'est de cette Semence que les Espaniols font la celebre Boisson de Chocolat. **Oexmelin** Histoire des Avanturers, ***Tom. 1. pag. 423***. He confirms more plainly the same Fancy, ***Pag. 426***.

CHAP. II.
Of the Choice and Disposition of the Place for Planting *Cocao-Trees*.

The *Cocao-Tree* grows naturally in several Countries in *America* under the Torrid Zone, but chiefly at *Mexico*, in the Provinces of *Nicaragua* and *Guatimala*, as also along the Banks of the River of the *Amazons*[n]. Likewise upon the Coast of *Caraqua*, that is to say, from Comana to Cartagena[o] and the *Golden Island*. Some also have been found in the Woods of *Martinico*.

The *Spaniards* and *Portuguese* were the first to whom the *Indians* communicated the Use of *Cocao-Nuts*, which they kept a long time to themselves without acquainting other Nations with it; who in reality know so little of it at this day, that some *Dutch* Corsairs, ignorant of the Value of some Prizes they had taken, out of contempt cast the Merchandize into the Sea, calling it in derision, in very indifferent *Spanish*, *Cacura de Carnero*[p], The Dung of Beasts.

In 1649[q] in the *Vert* Islands, they had never seen but one Tree planted, which was in the Garden of an *English-Man*, an Inhabitant of the Island of *St. Croix*[r]. In 1655, the *Caribeans*[s] shewed to M. *du Parepet* a *Cocao-Tree* in the Woods of the Island of *Martinico*, whereof he was Governour. This discovery was the Foundation of several others of the same kind, in the Woods of the *Cape Sterre*[t] of this Island. And it is probable that the Kernels which were taken out of them, were the Original of those *Cocao-Trees* that have been planted there since. A *Jew* named *Benjamin* planted the first about the Year 1660, but it was not till twenty or twenty-five Years after, that the Inhabitants of *Martinico* apply'd themselves to the Cultivation of *Cocao-Trees*, and to raise Nurseries of them.

When one would raise a Nursery, it is necessary, above all things, to chuse a proper Place, in respect of Situation, and a Soil agreeable to the Nature of it.

The Place should be level, moist, and not exposed to Winds; a fresh, and (if one may be allow'd the Expression) a Virgin Soil, indifferently fat, light, and deep. For this reason, Ground newly cleared, whose Soil is black and sandy, which is kept moist by a River, and its Borders so high as to shelter it from the Winds, especially towards the Sea Coast, is preferable to any other; and they never fail putting it to this Use, when they are so happy as to find any of this sort.

I have said, **Ground newly cleared**, that is to say, whose Wood is cut down purposely for it; for it is necessary to observe, that they at present plant their Nurseries in the middle of Woods, which have been so time out of mind, and this for two weighty Reasons: The First, because the Wood that is left standing round it, may serve as a Shelter; and the Second, because there is less Trouble in weeding or grubbing it. The Ground that has never produced any Weeds, will send forth but few, for want of Seed.

As for Nurseries planted in high Ground, the Earth is neither moist nor deep enough, and commonly the chief Root which grows directly downwards, cannot pierce the hard Earth which it soon meets with. Besides, the Winds are more boisterous, and cause the Blossoms to fall off as soon as blown, and when a little high, overturn the Tree, whose Roots are almost all superficial.

This is yet worse on the Hills, whose Descent is too steep; for besides the same Inconveniencies, the falling down of the Earth draws with it the good Soil, and insensibly lays the Roots bare.

One may therefore conclude that all these Nurseries are a long time before they bear, that they are never fruitful, and that they are destroy'd in a little time.

It is also proper that a Nursery, as much as may be, should be surrounded with standing Wood; but if it is open on any side, it should be remedy'd as soon as possible, by a Border of several Ranks of Trees called *Bananes*[5].

Besides this, the Nurseries should be moderate in respect of Magnitude, for the Small have not Air enough, and are, as it were, stifled; and the very Large are too liable to Dryness, and to the great Winds, which, in *America*, they call *Ouragans*[u].

The Place of the Nursery being chosen, and the Bigness determined, they apply themselves to clear it of the Wood. They begin with plucking up the little Plants, and by cutting the Shrubs, and small kinds of Trees, and felling the Trunks and larger Branches of others; they then make Piles, and set them on fire in all Parts, and so burn down the largest Trees of all, to save themselves the trouble of cutting them.

When all is burnt, and there remains nothing upon the Earth, but the Trunks of the great Trees which they don't trouble themselves to consume, and when the Space is well cleaned, they make Alleys by the help of a Line, strait and at equal Distances from each other, and thrust Sticks into the Ground of two or three Foot long, and 5, 6, 7, 8, 9 or 10 Feet distant, or at such a distance that they design to plant the *Cocao-Trees*, which they represent. Afterwards they plant *Manioc* in the empty Spaces, taking care not to come too near the Sticks.

One may observe, that the Nurseries planted at the great Distances of eight or ten Feet, are a great deal more troublesome to keep clean in the first Years, as we shall observe hereafter; but then they prosper a great deal better, bear more, and last longer.

The Inhabitants, who have a great deal to do, and have but few Slaves, plant the Trees nearer, because by this means they gain room, and they have less trouble to keep it clear; when afterwards the Trees come to hurt and annoy each other by their Proximity, and they have had some Crops to supply their present Necessities: or if otherwise, they are obliged to cut some to give Air to the rest.

On the Coast of *Caraqua*, they plant the *Cocao-Trees* at 12 or 15 Feet distance, and they make Trenches to water them from time to time in the dry Seasons. They happily experienced the Success of this Practice at *Martinico* some Years since.

The *Manioc*[6] is a woody Shrub, whose Roots being grated, and baked on the Fire, yield a *Cassave*, or Meal, which serves to make Bread for all the Natives of *America*. They plant it in the new Nurseries, not only because it is necessary to supply the *Negroes* with Food, but also it hinders the Growth of Weeds, and serves to shade the young *Cocao-Trees*, whose tender Shoots, and even the second Leaves, are not able to resist the scorching Beams of the Sun. For this reason they wait till the *Manioc* shades the Feet of the Sticks before they plant the *Cocao-Trees*, in the manner that we shall describe in the following Chapter.

NOTES:

[n] Relation of the River of the *Amazons*.
[o] I have added this Explication, because **Pomet** makes it come from ***Caraqua***, of the Province of ***Nicaragua*** in ***New Spain***, which is distant from ***Caracas*** 5 or 600 Leagues. V. VII. Chap. xiv.
[p] Thomas Gage, ***Tom. 1. Part 2. Chap. 19. Pag. 150.***
[q] Rochefort's ***Natural History of the*** Antilloes. ***Book 1. Chap. 6. Artic. 16.***
[r] Father ***Tertre***'s Hist. of the ***Antilloes***. Tom. 2. p. 184.
[s] These are the Savage Natives of the ***Antilloes***.
[t] That Part is call'd so, which lies exposed to the Winds which come always from the ***North-East*** to the ***South-East***. That Part under the Wind, is called ***Basse-Terre***.
[5] See the fifth Remark at the End of the Treatise.
[u] These violent and outrageous Winds blow from all Points of the Compass in twenty-four Hours. And this is one material thing to distinguish them from the regular and common Winds of this Climate.
[6] See the Remark at the sixth Article.

CHAP. III.
Of the Method of Planting a Nursery, and to cultivate it till the Fruit comes to Maturity.

Cocao-Trees are planted from the Kernel or Seed, for the Nature of the Wood will not admit of Slips: They open a *Cocao-Shell*, and according as they have occasion, take out the Kernels, and plant them one by one, beginning, for example, at the first Stick: They pluck it up, and with a sort of a Setting-Stick made of Iron, and well sharpened, they make a Hole, and turning the Iron about, cut off the little Roots that may do hurt. They plant the Kernel three or four Inches deep, and thrust in the Stick they before had pluck'd up a little on one side, to serve as a Mark: and so they proceed from Stick to Stick, and from Rank to Rank, till they have gone through the whole Nursery.

It must be observed, 1. ***Not to plant in a dry Season.*** One may indeed plant in any Month of the Year, or any Moon, new or old, when the Season is cool, and the Place ready; but it is commonly believed, that planting from *September* to *Christmas*, the Trees bear more than in some Months.

2. ***Not to plant any but the largest Kernels, and such as are plump***: For since in the finest Shells there are sometimes withered Kernels, it would be very imprudent to make use of them.

3. ***To plant the great Ends of the Kernels lowermost.*** This is that which is held by a little Thread to the Center of the Shell, when one takes the Kernel out. If the little End was placed downward, the Foot of the Tree would become crooked, neither would it prosper; and if it was placed sideways, the Foot would not succeed very well.

4. ***To put two or three Kernels at every Stick***, that if by any Mischance the

tender Shoots of one or two are broken by Insects, or otherwise, there may be one left to supply the Defect. If no bad Accident happen, you have the advantage of chusing the straitest and most likely Shoot. But it is not best to cut up the supernumerary ones till that which is chosen is grown up, and, according to all appearance, out of danger.

The Kernels come up in ten or twelve Days, more or less, according as the Season, more or less favourable, hastens or backens their Growth: The longish Grain of the Germ beginning to swell, sends forth the little Root downwards, which afterwards becomes the chief Stay of the Tree, and upwards it pushes out the Shoot, which is an Epitomy of the Trunk and the Branches. These Parts encreasing, and discovering themselves more and more, the two Lobes of the Kernel a little separated and bent back, appear first out of the Earth, and regain their natural Position, in proportion as the Shoot rises, and then separate themselves intirely, and become two Leaves of a different Shape, of an obscure Green, thick, unequal, and, as it were, shrivel'd up, and make what they call the *Ears* of the Plant. The Shoot appears at the same time, and is divided into two tender Leaves of bright Green: To these two first Leaves, opposite to each other, succeed two more, and to these a third Pair. The Stalk or Trunk rises in proportion, and thence forward during a Year, or thereabouts.

The whole Cultivation of the *Cocao-Tree* may then be reduced to the Practice of two Things.

First, To over-look them during the first fifteen Days; that is to say, to plant new Kernels in the room of those that do not come up, or whose Shoots have been destroy'd by Insects, which very often make dreadful Havock among these Plants, even when one would think they are out of danger. Some Inhabitants make Nurseries a-part, and transplant them to the Places where they are wanting: but as they do not all grow, especially when they are a little too big, or the Season not favourable, and because the greatest part of those that do grow languish a long time, it always seem'd to me more proper to set fresh Kernels; and I am persuaded, if the Consequences are duly weighed, it will be practised for the future.

Secondly, Not to let any Weeds grow in the Nursery, but to cleanse it carefully from one end to the other, and taking care, above all things, not to let any Herb or Weed grow up to Seed; for if it should happen so but once, it will be very difficult thenceforwards to root those troublesome Guests out, and to keep the Nursery clean, because the Cold in this Country never interrupts Vegetation.

This Weeding should be continued till the Trees are become large, and their Branches spreading, cast such a Shade as to hinder the Weeds from coming up; and afterwards, the Leaves falling from the Trees, and covering the Earth, will contribute to stifle them intirely. When this troublesome Business of Weeding is ended, it will be sufficient to overlook them once a Month, and pluck up here and there those few Weeds that remain, and to carry them far into the Woods for fear of Seeds.

When the *Cocao-Trees* are nine Months old, the *Manioc* should then begin to be pluck'd up; and it should be managed so, that in three Months time there should be none left. There may be a Row or two replanted in each Alley, and Cucumbers, Citruls, and [x] *Giraumonts* may be sow'd in the void Spaces, or *Caribean* Coleworts; because these Plants having great spreading Leaves, are very proper to keep the Earth cool and moist, and to stifle the noisome Weeds. When the *Cocao-Trees* come to shade the Ground entirely, then it will be necessary to pluck up every thing, for nothing then will grow beneath 'em.

The *Cocao-Trees* of one Year old have commonly a Trunk of four Feet high, and begin to spread, by sending out five Branches at the top, all at a time, which forms that which they call the *Crown* of a *Cocao-Tree*. It seldom happens that any of these five Branches are wanting, and if by any Accident, or contrary to the Order of Nature, it has but three or four, the Tree never comes to good, and it will be better to cut it off, and wait for a new Crown, which will not be long before it is form'd.

If at the end of the Year the *Manioc* is not plucked up, they will make the Trees be more slow in bearing; and their Trunks running up too high, will be weak, slender, and more exposed to the Winds. If they should be crowned, their Crowns will be too close; and the chief Branches not opening themselves enough, the Trees will never be sufficiently disengaged, and will not spread so much as they ought to do.

When all the Trunks are crowned, they chuse the finest Shoots, and cut up the supernumerary ones without mercy; for if this is not done out of hand, it will be difficult to persuade one's self afterwards: tho it is not possible but that Trees placed so near each other, should be hurtful to each other in the end.

The Trees are no sooner crown'd, but they send forth, from time to time, an Inch or two above the Crown, new Shoots, which they call Suckers: If Nature was permitted to play her part, these Suckers would soon produce a second Crown, that again new Suckers, which will produce a third, *&c.* Thus the **Cocao-Trees** proceed, that are wild and uncultivated, which are found in the Woods of **Cape-Sterre** in **Martinico**. But seeing all these Crowns do but hinder the Growth of the first, and almost bring it to nothing, tho it is the principal; and that the Tree, if left to itself, runs up too high, and becomes too slender; they should take care every Month when they go to weed it, or gather the Fruit, to prune it; that is to say, to cut or lop off all the Suckers.

I don't know whether they have yet thought it proper to prune, any more than to graft upon **Cocao-Trees**: There is however a sort of Pruning which, in my Opinion, would be very advantageous to it. These sort of Trees, for example, have always (some more than others) dead Branches upon them, chiefly upon the Extremities of the Boughs; and there is no room to doubt but it would be very proper to lop off these useless Branches, paring them off with the pruning Knife even to the Quick. But as the Advantage that will accrue from it will neither be so immediate, nor so apparent as the Time and Pains that is employ'd in it; it is very probable that this Care will be neglected, and that it will be esteem'd as Labour lost. But however, the **Spaniards** do not think so; for, on the contrary, they are very careful to cut off all the dead Sprigs: for which reason their Trees are more flourishing than ours, and yield much finer Fruit. I believe they have not the same care in grafting them, nor do I think any Person has hitherto attempted to do it: I am persuaded nevertheless, that the **Cocao-Trees** would be better for it. Is it not by the assistance of grafting our Fruit Trees in several manners, (which were originally wild, and found by chance in the Woods) that they have at length found the Art of making them bear such excellent Fruit?

In proportion as the **Cocao-Trees** grow, the Leaves upon the Trunks fall off by little and little, which ought to fall off on their own accord; for when they are entirely bare, they have not long to flourish: The first Blossoms commonly fall off, and the ripe Fruit is not to be expected in less time than three Years, and that if it be in a good Soil. The fourth Year the Crop is moderate, and the fifth it is as great as ever it will be; for then the Trees commonly bear all the Year about, and have

Blossoms and Fruit of all Ages. Some Months indeed there is almost none, and others, they are loaded; and towards the Solstices, that is, in *June* and *December*, they bear most.

As in the Tempests called ***Ouragans*** the Wind blows from all Points of the Compass in twenty-four Hours, it will be well if it does not break in at the weakest Place of the Nursery, and do a great deal of Mischief, which it is necessary to remedy with all possible expedition. If the Wind has only overturn'd the Trees without breaking the chief Root, then the best Method that can be taken in good Soil, is to raise them up again, and put them in their Places, propping them up with a Fork, and putting in the Earth about it very carefully: By this means they will be re-establish'd in less than six Months, and they will bear again as if no harm had come to them. In bad Soil, it will be better to let them lie, putting the Earth about the Roots, and cultivate at their lower Parts, or Feet, the best grown Sucker, and that which is nearest the Roots, cutting off carefully all the rest: The Tree in this Condition will not give over blossoming and bearing Fruit; and when in two Years time the Sucker is become a new Tree, the old Tree must be cut off half a Foot distant from the Sucker.

NOTES:

[x] These are Citruls whose Pulp is very yellow.

CHAP IV.
Of the gathering of the *Cocao-Nuts*, and the Manner of making them sweat, and of drying them that they may be brought sound into *Europe*.

The Observations which we made in the first Chapter, concerning the Alterations of the Colour of the Nuts, give us information of the time that they become ripe. It will be proper to gather them when all the Shell has changed Colour, and when there is but a small Spot below which shall remain green. They go from Tree to Tree, and from Row to Row, and with forked Sticks or Poles, they cause the ripe Nuts to fall down, taking great care not to touch those that are not so, as well as the Blossoms: They employ the most handy **Negroes** in this Work, and others follow them with Baskets to gather them, and lay them in Heaps, where they remain four Days without being touch'd.

    In the Months that they bear most, they gather them for a Fortnight together; in the less-fruitful Seasons, they only gather them from Month to Month. If the Kernels were left in Shells more than four Days, they would sprit, or begin to grow, and be quite spoiled[y]: It is therefore necessary to shell them on the fifth Day in the Morning at farthest. To do this, they strike on the middle of the Shells with a Bit of Wood to cleave them, and then pull them open with their Fingers, and take out the Kernels, which they put in Baskets, casting the empty Shells upon the Ground, that they may with the Leaves, being putrified, serve to fatten the Earth, and supply the Place of Dung.

    They afterwards carry all the Kernels into a House, and lay them on a heap upon a kind of loose Floor cover'd with Leaves of **Balize**[7], which are about four Feet long, and twenty Inches broad; then they surround it with Planks cover'd with the same Leaves, making a kind of Granary, which may contain the whole Pile of Kernels, when spread abroad. They cover the whole with the like Leaves, and lay some Planks over all: the Kernels thus laid on a heap, and cover'd close on all sides, do not fail to grow warm, by the Fermentation of their insensible Particles; and this is what they call *Sweating*, in those Parts.

They uncover the Kernels Morning and Evening, and send the *Negroes* among them; who with their Feet and Hands, turn them topsy turvy, and then cover them up as before, with the same Leaves and the same Planks. They continue to do this for five Days, at the end of which they have commonly sweat enough, which is discover'd by their Colour, which grows a great deal deeper, and very ruddy.

The more the Kernels sweat, the more they lose their Weight and Bitterness: but if they have not sweat enough, they are more bitter, and smell sour, and sometimes sprit. To succeed well therefore, there should be a certain Medium observed, which is only to be learnt by use.

When the Kernels have sweat enough, they lay them out to air, and expose them to the Sun to dry them, in the manner following.

They prepare before-hand, several Benches about two Foot high, in an even Court appointed for that purpose; they lay upon these Benches several Mats made of pieces of Reeds split in two, together with Bands made of *Mahot* Bark[8]. Upon these Mats they put the Kernels about two Inches in height and move and turn them very often with a proper Piece of Wood for the first two Days. At Night they wrap up the Kernels in the Mats, which they cover with *Balize* Leaves for fear of Rain, and they do the same in the day-time when it is likely to rain. Those who are afraid of having them stolen, lock them up.

There are some Inhabitants who keep Boxes about five Feet long, and two broad, and three or four Inches deep, on purpose to dry the Kernels: There is this Advantage in them, that in the greatest Rains and suddenest Showers, they may presently be piled one on the top of another, so that none but the top-most will want a Cover; which is soon done with the aforesaid Leaves, and an empty Box turn'd up-side down. But that which makes the Usage of Mats preferable, is, that the Air may pass through beneath, between the Partition of the Reeds, and so dry the Kernels better. Boxes whose Bottoms are made like a Sieve with strong Brass Wire, would be very excellent; but then they must be made in *Europe*, which would be a considerable Charge.

When the Kernels have sweat enough, they must be exposed upon the Mats as much as necessary: If Rain is foreseen that is likely to last, it will be best to let them sweat half a Day less. It is observable, that a few hours Rain at first, instead of doing any harm, makes them more beautiful, and better conditioned. In fair Weather, instead of this Rain, it will be proper to expose them to the Dew for the first Nights. The Rain of a whole Day or two will do no harm, if they are not covered before they have had the Benefit of the Sun, for a Day, or half a Day at least. For after a Day's Sun-shine, they are to be wrap'd in the Mat, as before directed; but if it be half a Day's Rain only, then they are only covered with **Balize** Leaves in the Night, kept on with little Stones laid at each End: But if the Rain be too long, it makes them split, and then they will not keep long; they therefore make Chocolate of it immediately.

If the Kernels have not sweat enough, or they wrap them too soon in the Mat, they are subject to sprit or germe, which makes them bitter, and good for nothing.

When the Kernels have been once wrapped in a Mat, and begun to dry, care must be taken that they do not grow moist again; they must therefore be well stirr'd from time to time, that they may be thorowly dry'd, which you may know by taking a Handful in your Hand, and shutting it: if it cracks, then it is time to put them into your Store-house, and to expose them to sale.

Those who would gain a Reputation in giving out a good Merchandize, before they pack it up in Vessels, pick it, and throw aside the little, wither'd, and thin Kernels, which are not only unsightly, but render the Chocolate something worse.

Afterwards the Kernels of the **Cocao-Nut** are dried in the Sun, before they are brought to **Europe**, and sold by the Druggists and Grocers, who distinguish it into great and small, and into that of **Caraqua**, and that of the **French** Islands, tho with no good Foundation, for in the Places themselves they make no mention of this Distinction: It therefore seems likely, that the Merchants find their account in sorting it, since Kernels proceeding from the same Tree, and from the same Nut, are not always of the same bigness. It is indeed true, that if one Parcel of Kernels be compared with another, the one may consist of bigger than the other, which may arise from the Age or Vigour of the Trees, or from the Nature of the Soil; but certainly there is no kind of Kernels which may be called Great, as a distinct Kind, nor consequently no other which can properly be said to be Small.

The Kernels that come to us from the Coast of *Caraqua*, are more oily, and less bitter, than those that come from the *French* Islands, and in *France* and *Spain* they prefer them to these latter: But in *Germany*, and in the North (*Fides sit penes Autorem*) they have a quite opposite Taste. Several People mix that of *Caraqua* with that of the Islands, half in half, and pretend by this Mixture to make the Chocolate better. I believe in the bottom, the difference of Chocolates is not considerable, since they are only obliged to encrease or diminish the Proportion of Sugar, according as the Bitterness of the Kernels require it. For it must be considered, as we have already said, that there is but one kind of *Cocao-Tree*, which grows as naturally in the Woods of *Martinico*, as in those of the Coast of *Caraqua*, that the Climates are almost the same, and consequently the Temperature of the Seasons equal, and therefore there cannot be any intrinsick Difference between these Fruits of any great moment.

As to the outward Difference that is observed, it can arise from nothing but the Richness of the Soil, or the contrary; from the different Culture, and from the Care or Negligence of the Labourers and those that prepare it, from the time of its gathering, to the time of its Delivery, and perhaps from all three together. It is to be observed at *Martinico*, that the *Cocao-Trees* prosper better in some Parts than others, merely from the Difference of the Soil, being more or less rich, or more or less moist.

I have had the Experience of one of my Friends, concerning what relates to the Cultivation and Preparation of this Tree and its Fruit, which demonstrates that they may add to its Value. This Gentleman, with a great deal of Application and Thought, found out the way to prepare the finest Merchandize of the Island, which was prefer'd by the Merchants to all the rest, and bore a greater Price than that of any of his Neighbours.

The Kernels of *Caraqua* are flattish, and for Bulk and Figure not unlike our large Beans. Those of *St. Domingo*, *Jamaica*, and *Cuba*, are generally larger than those of the *Antilloes*. The more bulky the Kernels are, and better they have been nourished, the less Waste there is after they have been roasted and cleansed, which some Years ago was an Advantage to those of *Caraqua*. But at present, by the Regulation from the Month of *April*, 1717, the Kernels of our Colonies pay but Twopence Duty for Entry, whereas Foreigners pay always Fifteen: These thirteen Pence difference make such ample amends for the small Waste, that there is a great deal of reason to hope, that for the time to come, there will be none but the Curious, and People that do not value the Expence, that will make use of the Chocolate of *Caraqua*, by way of preference to that of the *French* Islands, and that the Cheapness of the latter will double the Consumption at least.

The best ***Cocao-Nuts*** have very brown firm Shells, and when the Kernel is taken out, it ought to be plump, well nourish'd, and sleek; of the Colour of a Hazle-Nut on the outside, but more inclining to a Red within; its Taste a little bitter and astringent, not at all sour or mouldy[z]. In a word, without any Smell, and not worm-eaten.

The Fruit of the ***Cocao-Tree*** is the most oily that Nature has produced, and it has this admirable Prerogative, never to grow rank let it be ever so old, which all other Fruit do that are analogous to it in Qualities; such as ***Nuts***, ***Almonds***, ***Pine-Apple-Kernels***, ***Pistachoe Nuts***, ***Olives***, &c.

There are also imported from ***America***, ***Cocao-Kernel-Cakes*** of about a Pound weight each; and as this Preparation is the first and principal in the Composition of Chocolate, it will be proper to add here the Manner of making it.

The ***Indians***, from whom we borrow it, are not very nice in doing it; they roast the Kernels in earthen Pots, then free them from their Skins, and afterwards crush and grind them between two Stones, and so form Cakes of it with their Hands.

The ***Spaniards***, more industrious than the ***Savages***, and at this day other Nations after their Example, chuse out the best Kernels[a], and the most fresh: Of these they put about two Pounds in a great Iron Shovel over a clear Fire, stirring them continually with a large ***Spatula***, so long that they may be roasted enough to have their Skins come off easily, which should be done one by one[b], laying them a-part; and taking great heed that the rotten and mouldy Kernels be thrown away, and all that comes off the good ones; for these Skins being left among the Chocolate, will not dissolve in any Liquor, nor even in the Stomach, and fall to the bottom of Chocolate-Cups, as if the Kernels had not been cleansed.

If one was curious to weigh the Kernels at the Druggists, and then weigh them again after they are roasted and cleansed, one should find that there would be about a sixth Part wasted, more or less, according to the Nature and Qualities of the Kernels; that is to say, if you bought (for example) 30 Pounds, there would remain entirely cleansed, near twenty-five.

All the Kernels being thus roasted and cleansed at divers times, they put them once more to roast in the same Iron Shovel, but over a more gentle Fire, and stir them with the *Spatula* without ceasing till they are roasted all alike, and as much as they ought to be; which one may discover by their Taste, and their dark-brown Colour, without being black. The whole Art consists in avoiding the two Extremes, of not roasting them enough, and roasting them too much; that is to say, till they are burnt. If they are not roasted enough, they retain a disagreeable Harshness of Taste; and if they are roasted so much as to burn them, besides the Bitterness and ill Taste that they contract, they lose their Oilyness entirely, and the best part of their good Qualities.

In *France*, where they are very apt to run into Extremes, they are mighty fond of the burnt Taste, and the black Colour, as if they were proper Marks of good Chocolate, not considering that, Quantity for Quantity, they may as well put so much Charcoal as burnt Chocolate. This Opinion is not only agreeable to Reason and good Sense, but is also confirmed by the unanimous Consent of all that have written on this Subject; and I can affirm, that it is authorized by the universal Consent of all *America*.

When the Kernels are duly roasted, and well cleansed, they put them into a large Mortar to reduce them into a gross Powder, which they afterwards grind upon a Stone till it is very fine, which requires a more particular Explication.

They make choice of a Stone which naturally resists the Fire, not so soft as to rub away easily, nor so hard as to endure polishing. They cut it from 16 to 18 Inches broad, and about 27 or 30 long, and 3 in thickness, and hollowed in the middle about an Inch and a half deep. This Stone should be fix'd upon a Frame of Wood or Iron, a little higher on one side than the other: Under, they place a Pan of Coals to heat the Stone, so that the Heat melting the oily Parts of the Kernels, and reducing it to the Consistence of Honey, makes it easy for the Iron Roller, which they make use of for the sake of its Strength, to make it so fine as to leave neither Lump, nor the least Hardness. This Roller is a Cylinder of polish'd Iron, two Inches in diameter, and about eighteen long, having at each End a wooden Handle of the same Thickness, and six Inches long, for the Workman to hold by.

When the Paste is ground as much as is thought necessary, they put it hot in Moulds made of Tin, where they leave it, and it becomes hard in a very little time. The Shape of these Moulds is arbitrary, and every one may have them made according to his Fancy; but the cylindrick ones, which will hold about 2 or 3 Pounds of Chocolate, seem to me to be most proper; because the thicker they are, the longer they keep good, and may be commodiously held when there is occasion to scrape them. These Rolls ought to be wrapped in Paper, and kept in a dry Place: it should also be observed, that they are very susceptible of good and ill Smells, and that it is good to keep them 5 or 6 Months before they are used.

Now the Kernels being sufficiently rubb'd and ground upon the Stone, as we have just directed, if you would compleat the Composition in the Mass, there is nothing more to be done, than to add to this Paste a Powder sifted thro a fine Searce, composed of Sugar, Cinnamon, and, if it be desired, of **Vanilla** [c], according to the Quantities and Proportions, which we shall teach in the Third Part of this Treatise; and mix it well upon the Stone, the better to blend it and incorporate it together, and then to fashion it in Moulds made of Tin in the form of Lozenges of about 4 Ounces each, or if desired, half a Pound.

NOTES:

[y] For this reason, when they would send **Cocao-Nuts** to the neighbouring Islands from **Martinico**, that they may have wherewithal to plant, they are very careful not to gather them till the Transport Vessel is ready to sail, and to make use of them as soon as they arrive. For this reason also it is not possible that the Spaniards, when they design to preserve Nuts for planting, should let them be wither'd and perfectly dry, and that afterwards they should take the Kernels of these same Nuts, and dry them very carefully in the Shade, and after all, raise a Nursery with them, as **Oexmelin** reports, **History of Adventurers**, Tom. 1. Pag. 424.

[7] See the seventh Note hereafter.

[8] The **Mahot** is a Shrub, whose Leaves are round and feel soft like those

of ***Guimauve***; its Bark easily comes off, which they divide into long Slangs, which serves for Packthread and Cords to the Inhabitants and Natives.

[z] It gets this Taste either by being laid in a moist Place, or by being wet by Sea-Water in the Passage.

[a] As the Kernels are never so clean, but there may be Stones, Earth, and bad ones among them; it will be necessary, before they are used, to sift them in a Sieve that will let these things pass through, while it retains the Kernels.

[b] The Artists, to make this Work more expeditious, and to gain time, put a thick Mat upon a Table, and spread the Kernels upon it as they come hot from the Shovel, and roll a Roller of Iron over them to crack and get off the Skins of the Kernels; afterward they winnow all in a splinter Sieve, till the Kernels become entirely cleansed.

[c] What this is, you will find hereafter.

THE Natural HISTORY OF CHOCOLATE.
PART II.
Of the Properties of Chocolate.

We have hitherto treated of *Chocolate*, as it were, superficially, and as it presents itself to our Senses. We come next to examine its intrinsick Qualities, and to search into its Nature: As far as we can, we will discover what Reason, join'd to long Experience, has taught us concerning the salutary Properties of this Fruit.

CHAP. I.
Of the old Prejudices against Chocolate.

To proceed more methodically, and with greater Clearness in our Enquiries concerning *Chocolate*, it seems proper to set People right about the Prejudices which a false Philosophy has instilled into most Authors who have wrote upon this Subject; the Impressions whereof, are yet very deeply ingraven in the Minds of a great Number of People.

The *Spaniards*, who were first acquainted with Chocolate after the Conquest of the new World, have laid it down for an undoubted Truth, that *Chocolate* is cold and dry, participating of the Nature of Earth. They have supported this Determination neither with Reason nor Experience; nor do they know from whence they learnt it; perhaps they have taken it upon the Words, and from the Tradition of the Inhabitants of the Country. Let that be as it will, it is natural from false Principles to draw false Conclusions, of which the two principal are as follow.

The first is, That Chocolate being by Nature cold, it ought not to be used without being mixed with Spices, which are commonly hot, that so they might, both together, become temperate and wholesome. This was the Jargon and Practice of those Times. For the same Reason the ancient Physicians erroneously imagining that *Opium* was cold in the fourth Degree, never fail'd to correct this pretended Coldness in their narcotick Compositions, with Drugs extremely hot, as *Euphorbium*, *Pellitory*, *Pepper*, &c.

Their second Conclusion was, That Chocolate being dry and earthy, and from thence supposed to be of a styptick and astringent Quality; if it was not corrected, must necessarily breed Obstructions in the *Viscera*, and bring on a Cacochimy, and a great Number of other incurable Diseases.

These Prejudices have from the *Spaniards* pass'd into other Nations. To prove this, it will be unnecessary to cite a great Number of Authors, for whoever has read one, has read them all, the later having done nothing but copy the former; they have even sometimes improved their Dreams, and exaggerated this pretended Coldness of Chocolate, and at length push'd the Matter so far, as to make it a kind of cold Poison; and if it was taken to Excess, it would bring on a Consumption[1].

"Mexiaci friget nativa Cocai Temperies, tantoq; excedit Frigore ut inter noxia ne dubitem glandes censere Venena." *Thom. Strozzae* de Mentis potu seu de Cocolatis Opificio, *lib. 3*.

"Hinc siquis solo Cocolatis Fomite Vitam extrahat, atq; assueta neget Cibi Prandia, sensim contrahet exsueto marcentem Corpora Tabem."

It is not very extraordinary that People who are more ready to *believe* than to *examine*, (such as the World is full of) should give into the unanimous Opinion of so many Authors; and it would be strange if they were not carry'd down by the Stream of a Prejudice so general. But I cannot sufficiently admire that *Chocolate* being so much decry'd, has not been entirely laid aside as unfit for Use; without doubt there was nothing but the daily Experience of its good Effects, which could support it, and hinder it from giving way to Calumny.

Now to overturn this old System, it is sufficient, in my Opinion, to observe with how little Skill and Penetration they then treated of the whole Natural History; one ought not to be amazed that they have affirmed *Chocolate* to be cold and dry, in an Age when, for Example, they could say *Camphire* was cold and moist, which is a kind of Resin, from whence one Drop of Water cannot be extracted, whose sharp Taste, and penetrating Smell, joined to the extreme Volatility and Inflammability of its Particles, even in Water itself, are such evident Signs of its Heat, that it is difficult to conceive upon what account they persuade themselves of the contrary.

The Qualities of Chocolate are not indeed so remarkable, nor so active, as those of Camphire; but, with the least Attention, one may easily discern, that the Quantity of Oil that it contains, and the Bitterness that is perceivable in Tasting, are not the Marks of Coldness, since all Bitters are esteem'd hot, and since Oil is a Matter very near a-kin to, and necessary for Fire. This is very near the Reasoning of a celebrated Physician at *Rome* [2] against the old Opinion: *As for me*, says he, *I am of another Judgment; I believe that Chocolate is rather* temperate *than* cold, *and I refer my self to the Decision of every ingenious Person that will be at the pains to taste and examine it.*

These Reflections will be farther confirmed in the first Section of the following Chapter, where we shall experimentally demonstrate that Chocolate is a Substance very temperate, yielding soft and wholesome Nourishment, incapable of doing any Harm. And if this intrinsick Coldness is no more to be feared, it must be own'd, that it will be henceforward ridiculous, if not pernicious, to join it with hot acrid Spices, more likely to alter and destroy its good and real Qualities, than to correct the bad ones which it has not: I nevertheless do not doubt but the Pleasantness of the Smell, and the favourite Taste of several agreeable Spices, being pretty much liked in this Mixture, will have their Partizans; who, more delighted with a present Gratification, than afraid of the insensible Prejudice that these Ingredients bring to their Health, will not resolve to leave them off. Tho these will be no longer the Correctors of Chocolate, yet they will serve to season it, with which they will please their Taste, without troubling themselves with the Consequences. But those Persons who will give themselves the trouble of thinking, and are more tractable and less sensual, will wisely abstain from such Extreams, and their Moderation will not be unattended with Benefit. Health is so valuable a Blessing, that the Care to gain and preserve it, ought to supersede any other Consideration.

As to the pretended Obstructions which Chocolate is said to occasion from its astrictive Quality, they are so far from being afraid of it in *America*, that they have found by Experience a Vertue directly contrary to it; for several young Women, subject to the Whites, have been cured of this Distemper, by eating a Dozen *Cocao* Kernels for Breakfast every Morning. It is well enough known that Obstructions are the Cause of this Disease, which instead of being encreas'd by Chocolate, were entirely taken away.

Then as to those strange Disorders which are said to arise from its immoderate Use, we shall bring in the Sequel so many Facts directly contrary to these Chimerical Fears, that all Persons of good Sense will be disabused, and convinced of the salutary and wonderful Properties of this Fruit; which shall be the Subject of the following Chapter.

NOTES:

[1] **Ludov. Ramira**, Relat. ad Hurtad. ad Append. cap.
[2] **Paulus Zachias**, de Malo Hypocondriaco, Lib. 2. Cap. 15.

CHAP. II.
Of the real Properties of Chocolate.

Without talking in the Dialect of the *Peripateticks*, about the Qualities of Heat and Coldness, now-a-days so much decry'd, it will not be difficult to prove that Chocolate is a Substance, 1. Very temperate. 2. Very nourishing, and of easy Digestion. 3. Very proper to repair the exhausted Spirits and decayed Strength. 4. **Lastly**, Very suitable to preserve the Health, and prolong the Lives of old Men. These four Articles shall be sufficiently demonstrated in the four following Sections.

SECT. I.
Chocolate is very Temperate.

Nothing is so great an Argument that *Wheat*, *Rice*, *Millet*, and *Manioc*, are salutary and temperate, as their being used by whole Nations together. If any of these Substances had any predominant evil Quality, it would soon appear to the Prejudice of the Health of Numbers; the People who subsist upon it, would soon leave it off as a very dangerous and hurtful Aliment.

One may reason much after the same manner with respect to Chocolate. The Natives of *New-Spain*, and of a great part of the Torrid Zone of *America*, have always used it as a Delicacy; and at this day all the *European* Colonies which are establish'd in those Countries, make a Consumption of vast Quantities of it: These People use it at all Times, and in all Seasons, as constant daily Food, without regard to Age, Sex, Temperament, or Condition, without Complaint of having received the least Prejudice from it; they find on the contrary that it quenches Thirst, is very refreshing and feeding; that it procures easy quiet Sleep, and produces several other good Effects, to say nothing of those we are going to treat of in the following Sections. I could produce several Instances in favour of this excellent Nourishment, but I shall content myself with two only, equally certain and decisive in the Proof of its Goodness. The first is an Experiment of Chocolate's being taken for the ***only*** Nourishment, made by a Surgeon's Wife of *Martinico*: She had lost by a very deplorable Accident her lower Jaw, which reduced her to such a Condition, that she did not know how to subsist; she was not capable of taking any thing solid, and not rich enough to live upon Jellies and nourishing Broths. In this Strait she determined to take three Dishes of Chocolate, prepared after the manner of the Country, one in the Morning, one at Noon, and one at Night. (There, Chocolate is nothing else but *Cocao* Kernels dissolved in hot Water, with Sugar, and season'd with a Bit of Cinnamon.) This new way of Life succeeded so well, that she has lived a long while since, more lively and robust than before this Accident.

I had the second Relation from a Gentleman of *Martinico*, and one of my Friends, not capable of a Falsity. He assured me, that in his Neighbourhood, an Infant of four Months old unfortunately lost his Nurse, and its Parents not being able to put it to another, resolved through Necessity to feed it with *Chocolate*; the Success was very happy, for the Infant came on to a Miracle, and was neither less healthy nor less vigorous than those who are brought up by the best Nurses.

The Inferences that may be drawn from these two Histories are evident, and demonstratively prove that Chocolate has neither any intemperate nor hurtful Quality; I shall therefore say no more upon them, leaving every one to make his own proper Reflections.

SECT. II.
Chocolate is very nourishing and of easy Digestion.

This Proposition is a necessary Consequence of the foregoing, established by Facts which I have just related; and we have Experiments as convincing of its easy

Digestion, and the Goodness of the Chyle that it makes; but it needs no other Proof than the good Condition it puts those in, who ordinarily make use of it.

A learned *Englishman* has carried his Commendations so high concerning this particular Property of Chocolate, that he has not scrupled to affirm in a Dissertation that he has publish'd upon this Subject, That one Ounce of Chocolate contains as much Nourishment as a Pound of Beef. As much out of the way as this Assertion seems to be, one may easily conceive, that any Aliment is capable of yielding more plentiful Nourishment, if compar'd with any other, not only in respect to the Quantity, but also with relation to the Time that the Stomach takes to digest it.

Physicians are not agreed about the Causes of Digestion, but are divided into two Opinions, each of which is supported by the Writings of very eminent Authors; convinced of my own Inability to decide the Controversy, which also requires a large Field to expatiate in, I shall not undertake to defend either Fermentation or Trituration: But it will be sufficient to say, in two Words, that these Opinions are not absolutely incompatible[1]: it perhaps will not be difficult to make a sort of an Alliance or Agreement between them, by uniting whatever is plain and evident in the two Systems, and rejecting what is otherwise; and from hence form a third, which will be nothing but the Union of the uncontested Parts of the other two.

These two Causes undoubtedly concur in the Alteration that the Aliment undergoes in the Mouth; for the *Saliva* that mixes with it in Mastication, and dilutes it, cannot be deny'd to be an admirable Ferment[2]; and the Tongue which moves it, and the Teeth which grind it, and break it, must be own'd to be the first Instruments of Trituration.

Now since Nature is commonly uniform in her Operations, and since there is a great deal of reason to suppose that Nature compleats Digestion by the same means that she has begun it, let us suppose it is really so for a Moment, and apply it to the present Subject, and then we shall see by what Evidence Chocolate ought to be of an easy Digestion.

In the first place, bitter and alkaline Substances, such as these Kernels, are stomachick and analogous to the *Saliva* and the Ferment which dissolves the Aliment in the Stomach; how then can it be of hard Digestion with these Qualities?

In the second place, if one considers attentively the Kernels as they are roasted, broke, and ground extremely fine upon a Stone, afterwards melted and dissolved in boiling Liquor, which serves as a Vehicle for it; it then seems very likely that the Stomach will not have much Labour left to do. In short, by it Digestion is more than half finished.

Experience confirms these Reasonings very much, for the Digestion of Chocolate is soon brought about without Trouble, without Difficulty, and without any sensible rising of the Pulse; the Stomach very far from making use of its Strength, acquires new Force. And I can farther say, upon my own Knowledge, that I have seen several Persons who had but weak Digestion, if not quite spoiled, who have been entirely recovered by the frequent Use of Chocolate.

SECT. III.
Chocolate speedily repairs the dissipated Spirits and decay'd Strength.

If Chocolate did not produce this Effect, but only as it is very nourishing, it would but have this Property in common with the most juicy Aliments, and such as are most proper to furnish a good Quantity of Blood and Plenty of Spirits: but its Effects are far more speedy; for if a Person, for Example, fatigued with long and hard Labour, or with a violent Agitation of Mind, takes a good Dish of Chocolate, he shall perceive almost instantly, that his Faintness shall cease, and his Strength shall be recovered, when Digestion is hardly begun. This Truth is confirmed by Experience, tho' not so easily explained by Reasoning, because Chocolate sensibly appears to be soft, heavy, and very little disposed by any active Quality to put the Spirits in motion; however, being resolved to neglect nothing that is likely to unfold the Cause of an Effect so wonderful, I undertook one day the ***Chymical Analysis*** of Chocolate, and altho' prejudiced that I should discover nothing this way but a superficial Knowledge, yet I was willing to flatter myself that my Enquiry would not be wholly fruitless.

I cleansed sixteen Ounces of Kernels without burning them, I ground them in a Marble Mortar, and afterwards put them in a Glass Retort well luted; I placed it in a Reverberatory Furnace, and fixed to it a large Receiver; and after having luted the

Joints well, I gave it the first Degree of Fire.

The first that ascended was pure Phlegm, which dropt for about two Hours; a little white unctuous Matter swam on the top of it.

The Fire being augmented, the Drops became red, and congealed as they fell into the Receiver; this lasted about two Hours.

The Fire being again augmented, the Receiver was filled with white Clouds, which I saw resolve into a kind of Dew, white and unctuous, which was partly Spirit, and partly a white Oil; the red Drops however continued to the End, which was about two Hours and a half.

This Operation let me know that Chocolate contains two kinds of Oil; the one Red and Fixed, which congealed it self on the side of the Vessel; and the other White and Volatile, which proceeded from the white Clouds, and resolved itself on the other side of the Receiver.

On the Morrow after, having unluted the Receiver, and having placed it *in Balneo Mariae*, to melt the congealed Matter, I was agreeably surpriz'd to see the Vessel immediately fill'd with white Clouds: I very much admired the Volatility of this Unctuosity, and I was fully convinced, that Chocolate contained that *volatile Oil* so highly esteemed in Medicine, and that one need not go farther to seek the Cause of the speedy Reparation of the fainting Spirits; which is confirmed by the daily Experience of those that use Chocolate.

Having separated the Spirit by filtring through brown Paper, I divided the butirous Matter into two Parts: I put one, without any Addition, into a little Glass Cucurbit, which I placed in a Sand-Heat to rectify it, and by this Operation I got an Oil of an Amber Colour, swimming upon a little Phlegm, or Spirit[3].

I melted the remaining Part, and having incorporated it with quick Lime, I put it into a little Glass Retort luted, and put Fire to it by degrees. There first came over a clear Oil, the white Clouds succeeded, and at length the reddish Butter. Having unluted the Recipient, and put all in a little Cucurbit in a Sand-Heat, the white Clouds yielded an Oil of an Amber Colour; and having augmented the Fire, there came over a little red Oil, but no Spirit.

The Amber-coloured Oil is nothing else but the white volatile Oil, coloured a little by the Violence of the Fire: As for the red Oil, it seems to be the Remainder of the red Butter, fit to be exalted. These two Oils will not mix together; for the red, more fixed than the other, always gets to the bottom. Mr. Boyle[54] said he extracted from Human Blood, two Oils very like those above mentioned; and this Conformity of Substances, very much convinces me of the great Analogy I always supposed to be between Chocolate and Human Blood.

As for the Spirit, it has nothing very disagreeable either in Taste or Smell, it does not sensibly ferment with Alkalies, nor alters the Colour of blue Paper; after some time, it grows a little acid, and tastes a little tartish.

Having calcined the *Caput Mortuum*, which is of a violet Colour and filtred and evaporated the *Lixivium*, as is usual; I got nothing from it but a kind of Cynder, a little saltish, and in so small a quantity, that I did not give myself the trouble to reiterate the Calcination, Dissolution, Filtration, and Evaporation; for I should hardly have got five or six Grains of fixed purified Salt.

I curiously observed, that neither in the Heads, nor in the Receivers, there did appear any signs of a volatile Salt: However, *M. Lemery* assures us[55], that it contains a good deal; but it is plain he took his Opinion upon trust, for had he made the Experiment, he is too ingenious to be mistaken.

One may then conclude from these two Observations, That Chocolate is a mix'd Body, that has the least Quantity of Salt enters its Composition.

SECT. IV.
Chocolate is very proper to preserve Health, and to prolong the Life of Old Men.

Before Chocolate was known in *Europe*, good old Wine was called the Milk of old Men; but this Title is now apply'd with greater reason to Chocolate, since its Use has become so common, that it has been perceived that Chocolate is, with respect to them, what Milk is to Infants. In reality, if one examines the Nature of Chocolate, a little with respect to the Constitution of aged Persons, it seems as though the one was made on purpose to remedy the Defects of the other, and that it is truly the *Panacea* of old Age.

Our Life, as a famous Physician[56] observes, is, as it were, a continual growing dry; but yet this kind of natural Consumption is imperceptible to an advanced Age: when the radical Moisture is consumed more sensibly, then the more balmy and volatile Parts of the Blood are dissipated by little and little, the Salts disengaging from the Sulphurs, manifest themselves, the Acid appears, which is the fruitful Source of Chronick Diseases. The Ligaments, the Tendons, and the Cartilages have scarce any of the Unctuosity left, which render'd them so supple and so pliant in Youth. The Skin grows wrinkled as well within as without; in a word, all the solid Parts grow dry or bony.

One may say that Nature has formed Chocolate with every Vertue proper to remedy these Inconveniences. The volatile Sulphur with which it abounds, is proper to supply the Place of that which the Blood loses every day through Age, it blunts and sheaths the Points of the Salts, and restores the usual Softness to the Blood, like as Spirit of Wine united with Spirit of Salt, makes a soft Liquor of a violent Corrosive. This same sulphurous Unctuosity at the same time spreads itself in the solid Parts, and gives them, in some sense, their natural Suppleness; it bestows on the Membranes, the Tendons, the Ligaments, and the Cartilages, a kind of Oil which renders them smooth and flexible. Thus the ***Equilibrium*** between the Fluids and the Solids is in some measure re-establish'd, the Wheels and Springs of our Machine mended, Health is preserved, and Life prolonged. These are not the Consequences of Philosophical Reflections, but of a thousand Experiments which mutually confirm each other; among a great Number of which the following alone shall suffice.

> There lately died at **Martinico** a Counsellor about a hundred Years old, who, for thirty Years past, lived on nothing but Chocolate and Biscuit. He sometimes indeed had a little Soop at Dinner, but never any Fish, Flesh, or other Victuals: He was, nevertheless, so vigorous and nimble, that at fourscore and five, he could get on horseback without Stirrups.

Chocolate is not only proper to prolong the Life of aged People, but also of those whose Constitution is lean and dry, or weak and cacochimical, or who use violent Exercises, or whose Employments oblige them to an intense Application of Mind, which makes them very faintish: to all these it agrees perfectly well, and becomes to them an altering Diet.

On the contrary, I would not counsel the daily Use of it to such who are very fat, or who are wont to drink a good deal of Wine, and live upon a juicy Diet, or who sleep much, and use no Exercise at all: In a word, who lead a delicate, sedentary, and indolent Life, such as a great many People of Condition at *Paris* are used to. Such Bodies as these, full of Blood and Juice, have no need of additional Nourishment, and the Diet will fit them better which is mentioned in Ecclesiast. Plentiful Feeding brings Diseases, and Excess hath killed Numbers; but the temperate Man prolongs his Days[59].

NOTES:

[1] The ***Translator*** of this Treatise, who is a Physician, thinks it proper to observe, that the Opinions about Digestion, are deficiently related by our Author; for they are chiefly four, ***Trituration***, ***Fermentation***, ***Heat***, and by a ***Menstruum***, which are so far from being incompatible, that three of them necessarily concur to promote Digestion; to wit, ***Heat***, and a ***Menstruum*** or ***Liquor***, and ***Trituration***, or the Motion or rubbing of the Coats of the Stomach: For it is plain, if the two former are absent, there can be no Digestion, and without doubt the last does assist, but which is the principal, I shall not take upon me to determine.

[2] Our Author seems here either to mistake ***Ferment*** for ***Menstruum***, or to make them synonymous Terms: With this Allowance, his Reasoning is undoubtedly just; but as for a Ferment, in the usual Sense of that Word, it may justly be questioned whether there be any such in a Human Body.

[3] Our Author seems to make Phlegm and Spirit synonymous Terms in Chymistry.

[54] Pluribus abhinc Annis cum Sanguinem conveniente admodum digestione, praeparassem, & solicite distillatos Liquores supereffluentes flamma lampadis rectificassem: Inter alia duo obtinui olea diversi omnino Coloris, quorum alterum Flavedinem, aut pallorem Succini, alterum vero intensissimam Rubedinem imitabatur; illud autem ingeniosis etiam, lynceisq; Spectatoribus, miraculi instar erat, quod licet ambo haec Olea ab eodem

sanguine emanassent, forentq; pura satis & limpida, non tantum distinctis in Massis sibi invicem supra innatarent, sed si agitatione commiscerentur, paulatim sese mutuo iterum extricarent, ut Oleum & Aqua. ***Historia Sanguinis Humani.***

[55] Traite de Drogues, ***Pag. 127***.

[56] Baglivius in Edit. Lugd. 1709. ***Pag. 414.*** Vivere enim nostrum siccessere est.

[59] ***Chap.*** xxxvii. ***V.*** 33 & 34. In multis Escis erit Infirmitas, propter crapulam multi obierunt: Qui autem abstinens est, adjiecit Vitam.

THE Natural HISTORY OF *CHOCOLATE*.
PART III.
Of the Uses of Chocolate.

The common Uses of Chocolate may be reduced to three: It is put in Confections; it is used in Chocolate, properly so call'd; and there is an Oil drawn from it, to which they give the Name of Butter. I shall treat of them distinctly, in the three following Chapters.

CHAP. I
Of Chocolate in Confections.

They chuse **Cocao-Nuts** that are half ripe, and take out the Kernels one by one, for fear of spoiling them; they then lay them to soak for some Days in Spring Water, which they take care to change Morning and Evening: afterwards, having taken them out and wiped them, they lard them with little Bits of Citron-Bark and Cinnamon, almost as they make the Nuts of *Rouen*.

In the mean time, they prepare a Syrup of the finest Sugar, but very clear; that is to say, wherein there is but little Sugar: and after it has been clarified and purified, they take it boiling-hot off the Fire, and put in the **Cocao-Kernels**, and let them lie 24 Hours. They repeat this Operation six or seven times, encreasing every time the Quantity of Sugar, without putting it on the Fire, or doing any thing else to it: last of all, they boil another Syrup to the Consistence of Sugar, and pour it on the Kernels well wiped and put in a clean earthen Pot; and when the Syrup is almost cold, they mix with it some Drops of the Essence of Amber.

When they would have these in a dry Form, they take them out of the Syrup; and after it is well drained from them, they put them into a Bason full of a very strong clarify'd Syrup, then they immediately put it in a Stove, or Hot-House, where they candy it.

This Confection, which nearly resembles the Nuts of *Rouen*, is excellent to strengthen the Stomach without heating it too much; for this reason, they may safely be given to those who are ill of a Fever.

CHAP. II.
Of Chocolate, properly so called.

In treating of this Liquor, we have two things to examine: The First is, the Original of Chocolate, and the different Manner of preparing it: The Second, the Medicinal Uses that it is proper for; which shall be the Subject of the two following Sections.

SECT. I
Of the Original of Chocolate, and the different Manners of preparing it.

Chocolate is originally an *American* Drink, which the *Spaniards* found very much in use at *Mexico*, when they conquer'd it, about the Year 1520.

The *Indians*, who have used this Drink time out of mind, prepared it without any great Art; they roasted their Kernels in earthen Pots, then ground them between two Stones, diluted them with hot Water, and season'd them with *Pimento* [1]: those who were more curious, added *Achiota* [2] to give it a Colour, and [3] *Attolla* to augment its Substance. All these things joined together, gave to the

Composition so strange a Look, and so odd a Taste, that a *Spanish* Soldier said, it was more fit to be thrown to Hogs[4], than presented to Men; and that he could never have accustomed himself to it, if the want of Wine had not forced him to it, that he might not always be obliged to drink nothing but Water.

The *Spaniards*[5] taught by the *Mexicans*, and convinced by their own Experience, that this Drink, as rustick as it appeared to them, nevertheless yielded very wholesome Nourishment; try'd to make it more agreeable by the Addition of Sugar, some Oriental Spices, and Things that grew there, which it will be needless to mention, because the Names of them are not so much as known here, and because of so many Ingredients, there is none continued down to us but *Vanilla*; in like manner, that Cinnamon[6] is the only Spice which has had general Approbation, and remains in the Composition of Chocolate.

Vanilla is a Cod of a brown Colour and delicate Smell; it is flatter and longer than our [*French*] Beans, it contains a luscious Substance, full of little black shining Grains. They must be chosen fresh, full, and well grown, and care must be taken that they are not smeared with Balsam, nor put in a moist Place.

The agreeable Smell, and exquisite Taste that they communicate to Chocolate, have prodigiusly recommended it; but long Experience having taught that it heats very much, its Use is become less frequent, and those who prefer their Health more than pleasing their Senses, abstain from it entirely. In *Spain* and *Italy*, Chocolate prepared without *Vanilla*, is called at present *Chocolate of Health*; and in the *French* Islands of *America*, where *Vanilla* is neither scarce nor dear, as in *Europe*, they do not use it at all, though they consume as much Chocolate there as in any other Place in the World.

However, a great many People are prejudiced in favour of *Vanilla*, and that I may pay a due Deference to their Judgments, I shall employ *Vanilla* in the Composition of *Chocolate*, in the best Method and Quantity, as it appears to me; I say, as it appears to me, because there are an infinite Variety of Tastes, and every one expects that we should have regard to his, and one Person is for adding what the other rejects. Besides, when it is agreed upon what things to put in, it is not possible to hit upon Proportions that will be universally approved; it will therefore be sufficient for me to make choice of such Things as the Majority are agreed upon, and consequently which are agreeable to the Tastes of most.

When the Chocolate Paste is made pretty fine upon a Stone, as I have already explain'd, they add Sugar powdered and passed through a fine Searce; the true Proportion is the same Weight of Sugar as of Kernels, but it is common to put a quarter part less of the former, that it may not dry the Paste too much, nor make it too susceptible of Impressions from the Air, and more subject to be eaten by Worms. But this fourth Part is again supply'd, when it is made into a Liquor to drink.

The Sugar being well mix'd with the Paste, they add a very fine Powder made of *Vanilla* and *Cinnamon* powdred and searced together. They mix all over again upon the Stone very well, and then put it in Tin Moulds, of what Form you please, where it grows as hard as before. Those that love Perfumes, pour a little Essence of Amber on it before they put it in the Moulds.

When the Chocolate is made without *Vanilla*, the Proportion of Cinnamon is two Drams to a Pound of Paste; but when *Vanilla* is used, it should be less by one half. As for the *Vanilla*, the Proportion is arbitrary; one, two, or three Cods, and sometimes more, to a Pound, according to every one's Fancy.

Those that make Chocolate for Sale, that they may be thought to have put in a good deal of *Vanilla*, put in Pepper, Ginger, *&c.* There are even some People so accustomed to these Tastes, that they will not have it otherwise; but these Spices serving only to inflame the Blood, and heat the Body, prudent People take care to avoid this Excess, and will not use any Chocolate whose Composition they are ignorant of.

Chocolate made after this manner, has this Advantage, that when a Person is obliged to go from Home, and cannot stay to have it made into Drink, he may eat an Ounce of it, and drinking after it, leave the Stomach to dissolve it.

In the *Antilloes* they make Cakes of the Kernels only, without any Addition, as I have taught at the End of the first Part of this Treatise; and when they would make Chocolate of them, they proceed in the following Manner.

NOTES:

[1] [2] [3] See the Remarks 8, 9, and 10.
[4] Porcorum ea verius Colluvies quam hominum Potio. *Benzo* apud *Clu-*

sium Exoticorum Lib. Cap. 28.
[5] Haec olim Cocolatis erant Exordia & Artis prima Rudimenta. *P. Thomae Strozzae* de Mentis potio.
[6] See the 11th Remark.

The Method of making Chocolate after the
Manner of the *French* Islands in *America*.

They scrape off with a Knife from these Cakes aforesaid[1], what Quantity they please, (for Instance, four large Spoonfuls, which weigh about an Ounce) and mix with it two or three Pinches of powder'd Cinnamon finely searced, and about two large Spoonfuls of Sugar in Powder[2].

They put this Mixture into a Chocolate-Pot with a new-laid Egg[3], both White and Yolk; then mix all well together with the Mill, and bring it to the Consistence of Liquid Honey, upon which they afterwards pour boiling Liquor[4], (Milk or Water, as is liked best) at the same time using the Mill that they may be well incorporated together.

Afterwards they put the Chocolate-Pot on the Fire, or in a Kettle of boiling Water; and when the Chocolate rises, they take it off, and having well mill'd it, they pour it into the Dishes. To make the Taste more exquisite, one may, before it is poured out, add a Spoonful of Orange-Flower Water, wherein a Drop or two of Essence of Amber has been put.

This Manner of making Chocolate has several Advantages above any other, and which render it preferable to them all.

In the first place, one may assert, that being well managed, it has a very agreeable Smell, and a peculiar Delicacy in the Taste; besides, it passes very easily off the Stomach, nor leaves any Settling either in the Chocolate-Pot, or in the Dishes.

In the second place, one has the Satisfaction to prepare it one's self to one's own Taste, to encrease or diminish at pleasure the Quantities of Sugar or Cinnamon, and to add or leave out the Orange-Flower Water, or Essence of Amber; and, in a word, to make any other Alteration that shall be most agreeable.

In the third place, they make no Additions that destroy the good Qualities of the Kernels; it is so temperate, that it may be taken at all Times, and by all

Ages, in Summer as well as in Winter, without fearing the least Inconveniency: Whereas *Chocolate* season'd with *Vanilla*, and other hot and biting Ingredients, cannot but be very pernicious, especially in Summer, to young People, and to dry Constitutions. The Glass of cold Water that they have introduced to drink before it, or after it, only serves to palliate the Effects for a Time; for the Heat that attends it, will manifest itself in the Blood and *Viscera*, when the Water is drain'd off and gone, by the ordinary ways.

In the fourth place, a Dish is so cheap, as not to come to above a Penny. If Tradesmen and Artizans were once aware of it, there are few who would not take the Advantage of so easy a Method of Breakfasting so agreeably, at so small a Charge, and to be well supported till Dinner-time, without taking any other Sustenance, Solid or Liquid.

NOTES:

[1] Or rather grate it with a flat Grater, when the Cakes are so dry that they will not be so easily scraped with a Knife.
[2] Because if it was in a Lump, it would weigh more than double the Quantity of scraped Chocolate.
[3] The oily Parts of the Chocolate would not readily unite with the aqueous or watry Parts of the Liquor, without the Intervention of the Egg, which serves as a common Bond, without which this Drink would not have a good Head.
[4] The Proportion of Liquor should be about eight Ounces, or half a Pint, to one Ounce of Chocolate.

SECT. II.
Of the Uses that may be made of Chocolate with relation to Medicine.

I have always imagined it would be a very great Advantage to Physick, if Medicines could be administred to sick People under an agreeable Form, and a familiar

Taste; and the Artifice itself of giving any thing under the appearance and name of something that is delicate, is not without its Benefit: People afflicted with Distempers, have enough to do to support their Pains, without the Inconveniency of distasteful Remedies; however, it would be no small matter to spare them the Aversion they have to every thing that is called a Medicine; and when there is a Necessity for such, Chocolate may serve for very proper Diet, and an excellent Vehicle, wherein to take a Medicine at the same time.

These have been my Thoughts for some Time, and I can affirm that a happy Success has often confirm'd my Opinion. I could wish that this Essay, imperfect as it is, might serve to waken the Attention of some ingenious Physician, who would give himself the trouble to handle this Matter with greater Accuracy than my small Penetration will permit me to do.

1. How many People neglect to purge themselves, and are so obstinate as to refuse to do it, when they have the greatest need of it, and this because of the great Distaste they have for ordinary Medicines? Will it not be of the greatest Service to teach them to purge themselves after a delightful Method, and even, if it was necessary, to purge them without their knowledge? To do this, you need only mix 20 or 26 Grains of *Jalap* in Powder, (more or less, according to the Age and Strength of the Person) with so much Powder of Cinnamon as is common for a Dish of Chocolate, and to give this Dish as if it were ordinary Chocolate. I have had great Experience of this, it is a good Purge without Griping; several have mistaken the Effect for the Benefit of Nature only, being entirely ignorant of the officious Deceit which I made use of for their sakes. What Advantages may not there be drawn from this Method of Purging apply'd to Children, who are so backward to take any thing that has the least ill Taste?

2. The Preparations of the *Cortex*, both Galenical and Chymical, have not succeeded. Its Infusion in Wine, heretofore so much cry'd up, contains but a part of the Vertue; for the *Faeces*, or the Bark that remains at the bottom of the Bottle, has Strength enough to cure the intermitting Fever. Thus after a thousand fruitless Trials, it is now given again in Substance, reduced to a very fine Powder, which is either made into *Bolus's*, or taken in Water. This Practice however is attended with several Inconveniences; for a great many People, especially Children, cannot swallow it in *Bolus's*. The same Inconveniences follow the other Way of taking it

in Water, and is neither less troublesome, nor less nauseous.

To avoid all this, a Dram of the *Cortex* reduced to a fine[1] Powder, and finely searced, and afterwards ground dry on a Porphyry, with the Cinnamon designed for a Dish of Chocolate, and mixed in the Chocolate with more Sugar than ordinary, may be taken without the least Reluctancy, and, if necessary, without being perceived: The Person will be nourished at the same time much better than with Broth, which is easily corrupted by a feverish Stomach; neither will the Particles of the *Cortex* offend the Stomach, being wrapped up by the Unctuosity of the Chocolate. I have cured Intermittent Fevers after this manner, nor did it ever fail of good Success.

3. The most elaborate Preparations of Steel, are not one jot the better upon that account; the simple Filings have more Vertue than was ever extorted from this Metal by any Preparation: there is nevertheless an Inconveniency in the Use of them, because all the Particles of the Steel uniting together, by their Weight, at the bottom of the Stomach, form a kind of a Cake, which fatigues it, and makes it very uneasy.

To remedy this, after the Filings have been ground into a very fine Powder upon a Porphyry; you must mix it with the Cinnamon, when you make your Chocolate, and it is certain that the Particles of the Steel will be so divided and separated by the Agitation of the Mill, and so entangled in the Chocolate, that there will be no danger of a future Separation. Besides, the aromatick Particles of the Cinnamon, and the alkaline ones of the Chocolate, will not a little add to the Strength and Operation of this Remedy.

4. After this manner may you mix with the Chocolate the Powders of ***Millepedes***, ***Vipers***, ***Earthworms***, the Livers and Galls of Eels, to take away the distasteful Ideas that the Sick entertain against these Remedies.

5. The Use of Milk is a specifick Remedy for the Cure of several Distempers, but by Misfortune there are but few Stomachs that can bear it, and several Methods have been try'd to find out Help for this Inconvenience. Without troubling myself to mention or examine them, will it not be an easy and natural Method, to hinder the Milk from curdling on the Stomach, to pour a hot Dish of Chocolate upon a Pint or Quart of Milk? The butirous Parts of the Milk and Chocolate, are in reality analogous to each other, and very proper to be united for the same Purpose; and what is

bitter and alkaline in the Chocolate, ought necessarily to hinder the curdling of the Milk in the Stomach. It is easy to confirm by Experience the Reasoning upon this sort of Chocolated Milk.

NOTES:

[1] This, if true, overturns what has been said about the Mechanical Cure of an Ague, by *Quincy*, who pretends that the Vertue of the Cortex lies in its Texture, which this Preparation destroys.

CHAP. III.
Of the Oil or Butter of Chocolate.

Chocolate Kernels are a Fruit very oleaginous, but the Oil is very closely united with the other Principles, that it requires a great deal of Labour to separate it, and to make it pure. The three common Ways to extract Oils, are by Distillation, Expression, and Decoction; we reject the first as being very imperfect, because the Violence of the Fire alters the Nature of all Oils that are extracted that way. The Success will answer no better by Expression, because that which is got will be very impure and in very small Quantity. There then remains no way but by Decoction, to draw out this essential Oil that we are in quest of, which is the true and the only way, for it gives it in its utmost Purity without any Alteration.

They take Chocolate that is roasted, cleaned, and ground upon the Stone, they throw the Paste into a Pan of boiling Water over a clear Fire; they let it boil till almost all the Water is consumed, then they pour more Water upon it till the Pan is full; the Oil ascends to the Top in proportion as the Water cools, and grows to the Consistence of Butter. If this Oil is not very white, it needs only be melted in a Pan full of hot Water, where it will be disengaged and purified from the red and terrestrial Particles that remain.

At *Martinico* this Oil is of the Consistence of Butter, but brought into *France*, it becomes almost as hard as *Fromage*, or *French* Cheese, which melts nevertheless, and becomes liquid with a moderate Heat: it has no very sensible Smell, and has the good fortune never to grow rank; I have some of it now by me, that has been made this fifteen Years. One Year, when Oil of Olives failed us, we used that of Chocolate during the Time of **Lent**. It is very well tasted, and very far from being hurtful; it contains the most essential and most healthful Parts of the Chocolate.

I had the Curiosity to examine it by a Chymical Analysis; I put three Ounces into a little Glass Cucurbit placed in the Heat of Ashes, there drop'd from it an oily Liquor, which congealed as it fell down, and which did not differ from the Butter that I have described, but by a light Impression made upon it by the Fire. I only observed, that there was at the bottom of the Receiver, two or three Drops of a clear Liquor, which tasted a little acid, but very agreeable.

As this Oil is very anodyne, or an Easer of Pain, it is excellent, taken inwardly, to cure Hoarseness, and to blunt the Sharpness of the Salts that irritate the Lungs. In using, it must be melted and mix'd with a sufficient Quantity of Sugar-Candy, and made into Lozenges, which must be held in the Mouth as long as may be, before they melt quite away, swallowing it down gently.

Oil of Chocolate also taken seasonably, may be a wonderful Antidote against corrosive Poisons.

Its Vertues are no ways inferior, if used outwardly.

1. It is the best and most natural **Pomatum** for Ladies to *clear* and *plump* the Skin when it is *dry*, *rough*, or *shrivel'd*, without making it appear either *fat* or *shining*. The **Spanish Women** at **Mexico**, use it very much, and it is highly esteem'd by them. If it is thought too hard, it may be softened with Oil of Ben, or Oil of Sweet Almonds, cold drawn.

2. I am persuaded if the antient Custom of the **Greeks** and **Romans**, of anointing their Bodies with Oil, was revived, there is nothing would answer their Expectations better, in augmenting the Strength and Suppleness of their Muscles, and preserving them from Rheumatisms and other torturing Pains. The leaving off this Practice, can be attributed to nothing else but to the ill Smell and other Properties that attended it; but if Oil of Chocolate was used instead of Oil of Olives, those Inconveniences would be avoided, because it has no Smell, and dries entirely into the Skin: nothing certainly would be more advantageous, especially for aged Persons, than to renew this Custom, which has been authorized by the Experience of Antiquity.

3. Apothecaries ought to make use of this preferably to all others, as the Basis of their Apoplectick Balsams; because all other Oils grow rancid, and the Oil of Nutmegs, though whiten'd with Spirit of Wine, always retains somewhat of its natural Smell, whereas Oil of Chocolate is not subject to any of these Accidents.

4. There is nothing so proper as this to keep Arms from rusting, because it contains less Water than any other Oil made use of for that purpose.

5. In the *American* Islands they make use of this Oil to cure the Piles; some use it without Mixture, others melt two or three Pounds of Lead, and gathering the Dross, reduce it into fine Powder, and after it is finely searced, incorporate it with this Oil, and make a Liniment of it very efficacious for this Disease. Others for the same Intention mix with this Oil the Powder of *Millepedes*, Sugar of Lead, *Pompholix*, and a little *Laudanum*.

Others use this Oil to ease Gout Pains, applying it hot to the Part, with a Compress dip'd in it, which they cover with a hot Napkin. It may be used after the same manner for the Rheumatism.

6. *Lastly*, This Oil enters the Composition of the wonderful Plaister, and the *Pomatum* against Tetters. You will find their Description and Properties among the Remarks at the End of this Treatise.

REMARKS Upon some PLACES of the TREATISE upon *Chocolate*.

REMARK I.

The *Coco-tree* is the same as the Palm-Tree so famous in the *East-Indies*; its Fruit is call'd *Coco*, and care should be taken that it be not confounded with *Cocao*. I make this Remark, because I find that *William Dampier* very improperly calls[a] *Coco's Cocao-Nuts*, and the Tree that bears them a *Cocao*.

REMARK II.

They have transported these great Trees from *St. Domingo* to the *Vent Islands*; their Leaves being almost round, are firm and so smooth, that one would think they had been varnished. Their Fruit are sometimes as large as one's Head, and their Skins very thick: When that is taken off, the Pulp is very near the Colour, Smell, and Taste of our Apricocks; in the Middle there are four Stones as big as Pullets Eggs, which are difficult to separate from the Fruit. They are eaten with Wine and Sugar; they make also very good Marmalade.

REMARK III.

The ***Calebash***-Tree is nigh as large as the Apple-Tree; it supplies the Natives and Negroes with Buckets, Pots, Bottles, Dishes, Plates, and several other Houshold Utensils. One cannot describe the Shape nor Bigness of ***Calebashes***, since there are some of the Size of a Pear, and others as large as the greatest Citrons; and besides, there are long, round, oval, and of all Fashions. The Fruit, which is green and smooth upon the Tree, becomes grey as it dries; within, it is full of a white Pulp, of no use at all, which they take out through a Hole; the Shells they put to several Services. The Bark is about one Fifth of an Inch thick, but very hard, and difficult to break.

REMARK IV.

The ***Papaw***-Tree is pretty uncommon as to its Make; its Trunk is strait, but hollow, and of so tender a Wood, that it is easily cut down with a Hedging-Bill; it is about four Yards high, without any Branches; its Leaves much like those of our Fig-Trees, but twice as big, and are joined to the top by Stalks of a Foot and a half long, and hollow like a Reed. They being about thirty in number, grow at the top of the Trunk all round about it; the lowest are ripest and largest, they are green, and of the bigness of one's Fist. The Pulp, which is but half an Inch thick, is like that of a Melon, but of a sweet faintish Taste; but it makes a pretty good Confection, of a fine green Colour.

There is another kind of ***Papaw***-Tree, whose Fruit is as large as a Melon, and better tasted than the former.

REMARK V.

The ***Banane*** is a sort of Plant, whose Root is a great round Bulb, from whence proceeds a Trunk, green and smooth, six Feet high, as thick as one's Thigh, and without any Leaf. On the top of it grow about twenty Leaves, about a Foot and a half broad, and about five Feet long; but so tender, that the Wind tears them from the Middle to the Sides, into Slangs like Ribbons: From the Center of these Leaves grows a second Trunk, more firm than the rest of the Plant: upon this grows a Cluster of about forty or fifty ***Bananes***, sometimes more, sometimes less. A ***Banane*** is a Fruit as thick as one's Arm, about a Foot long, and a little crooked. They gather this Cluster green, and hang it up in the Ceiling; and as the ***Bananes*** grow yellow, or mellow, they gather them. When this Cluster is taken away, the Plant withers, or they cut it down at the Root; but for one Trunk lost, the Root sends forth five or six more.

Besides these *Bananes*, there is a Fruit call'd *Banane-Figs*; but the Plants that produce them are very little different: The Figs are much less than the *Bananes*, being but four or five Inches long. The Fig is more delicious, but the *Banane* is thought to be more wholesome, and the Pulp more solid. They roast them upon a Grid-Iron, or bake them in an Oven, they eat them with Sugar and the Juice of an Orange. The *Banane* done in a Stew-Pan in its own Juice, with Sugar and a little Cinnamon, is excellent.

REMARK VI.

Manioc is a Shrub very crooked, and full of Knots, its Wood is tender and brittle, and the Branches are easily broke off into Slips: There are several and different Colours, some more forward and fruitful than others. Commonly they are pluck'd up in a Year or thereabouts; and there is found at every one, several plump Roots, without any sensible Fibres, more or less thick, according to the Kind and the Goodness of the Soil. These Roots are wash'd in a good deal of Water, to free them from the Earth; and after they are scraped with a Knife like wild Turnips, they *grate* them; that is to say, they rub them hard with great Copper Graters, which the *French* call *Grages*, just as they do Quinces to get out the Juice. This grated *Manioc* is put in the Press in Sacks made of coarse Hemp, or Rushes, to get out the superfluous Moisture, which is not only unwholesome, but poisonous. This, thus press'd, they take from the Sacks, and pass it through a coarse Sieve called *Hibichet*; they afterwards bake it two several ways, to make what they call *Cassave*, or Meal of *Manioc*.

In the first place, when they would make the *Cassave*, they spread the sifted *Manioc* upon a Plate of Iron over a clear Fire, which they tapping down with the Ball of their Hands, make a broad Cake about half an Inch thick, and two Feet in diameter; and when it is baked on one side, they turn it on the other: and if they would keep it any time, they dry it in the Sun.

In the second place, when they would make what they call the Meal, they put the *Manioc*, grated, pressed, and sifted, as before, upon a great Copper Plate four Feet in diameter, with a Brim five or six Inches high, and placed upon a Brick Furnace: They stir it continually with a wooden *Spatula*, that it may not stick and be baked all alike. This Meal resembles Bread grosly crumbled, and may be kept a long while in a dry Place. The Natives do not trouble themselves to make the Meal; they only eat *Cassave*, which they bake every day, because, when it is hot, it is more agreeable and palatable.

If they leave the expressed Juice of *Manioc* to settle, it lets fall a *Faecula* to the bottom, called *Moussache*, which they afterwards dry in the Sun: it is as white as Snow, of which they make very good Cakes, called in those Parts, *Craquelins*.

The Laundresses use this *Faecula* instead of Starch, to starch their Linnen. Some Inhabitants mix one Third of this with two Thirds of *French* Meal, and make Bread that is very white, and well tasted.

REMARK VII.

At first sight, one would take a *Balize*-Tree for a *Banane*, they are so like each other: there is, however, this difference between them, That the Leaves of the *Balize*-Tree are not so tender, and apt to be tore; for this reason, they serve the Natives for Table-Cloths and Napkins, as well as the Negroes, and some of the Planters that live in the Woods. Sometimes they serve as Umbrella's to shade them from the Sun, or Showers of Rain, that surprize them.

The Hunters have great assistance from this Plant; for sometimes finding themselves pressed with Thirst, in Places at some distance from Rivers or Fountains, they give the Trunk of a *Balize* a Slash with a Knife, and immediately hold their Hat, or a Cup, which catches a clear, good, and cool Water, even in the greatest Heat.

REMARK VIII.

Pimento, called also *Jamaica-Pepper*, has been brought into *France*, where it grows, as in *America*, in pyramidal Cods of three or four Inches long: they are at first green, then yellow, afterwards red, and last of all, black. They pickle them in Vinegar, as they do Capers and little Cucumbers. There are in *America* several other Kinds of *Pimentoes*, and especially one that is round, and as red as a Cherry. This is the hottest of all, it sets the Mouth all on fire; for which reason it is called the mad *Pimento*. The Natives eat nothing without *Pimento*, it is their universal Seasoning, it serves them instead of Salt, and all Oriental Spices.

REMARK IX.

Achote is best known in *France*, under the Name of *Roucou*, and is a sort of Red which the Dyers and Painters make use of. It is the favourite Colour of the Savages, which they are very careful of planting in their Gardens, that they may paint their Bodies every Morning, which they call *Roucouing*.

Roucou is planted of a Kernel much after the same manner as the *Cocao-Tree*. The Shrub that is most like it in *Europe*, is the *Lilach*, or the *Arabian* Bean. Its Leaves, of the Shape of a Heart, are longish, pointed, and placed alternately; its Blossoms grow in Bunches at the end of the Boughs, they are white, mix'd with Carnation, like the Flowers of the wild Rose-Tree. In the middle, there is a Tuft of yellow *Stamina* with red Points; when these Blossoms fall off, there appears tawny Buds, beset with fine Prickles: These Buds grow to be Shells, which, when ripe, open on the upper side, and discover within, two Rows of Pippins, almost like little Peas, cover'd with Vermilion, which sticks to the Fingers, when touch'd, and leaves the Pippins quite, when wash'd with warm Water. The Water being settled, they pour it off gently by degrees, they dry the Colour in the Shade that fell to the bottom of the Vessel; and this is the true *Roucou*, without any Mixture. The Physicians in these Parts prescribe it to cut and attenuate thick and tough Humours, which cause difficulty of Breathing, Retension of Urine, and all sorts of Obstructions[89].

REMARK X.

Atolla is a kind of Gruel which they make with Meal of *Maise*, (which is the same as our *Indian* Corn, or *Turkey* Millet.) The *Mexicans* season it with *Pimento*; but the Nuns and *Spanish* Ladies, instead of *Pimento*, use Sugar, Cinnamon, perfumed Waters of Amber, Musk, *&c.* In these Parts, they make the same Use of *Atolla*, as of the best Rice in the *Levant*.

REMARK XI.

One ought to chuse the smallest Cinnamon, the highest coloured, and of the most biting Taste, as well as sweet and spicy, because a great Part is full of Pieces, from whence they have drawn the Essence, and has neither any Colour nor Taste, but that of the Wood. To help and amend both, there needs only a Clove to be ground in the Mortar, with an Ounce of Cinnamon. This Spice is best that comes from the *East-Indies*, it has nothing of Acrid in it, and contains an oleous Volatile, which agrees very well with that of Chocolate. Cinnamon also has always kept its Place in all the Compositions of Chocolate.

NOTES:

[a] *New Voyage round the World*, Tom. 1. Chap. 10.
[89] Thomas Gage, *Tom. 1. Part 2. Pag. 142*.

MEDICINES In whose Composition OIL or BUTTER OF CHOCOLATE Is made use of.

The Wonderful Plaister for the Curing of all sorts of Ulcers.
Take **Oil-Olive** a Pound, **Venetian Ceruss**, in Powder, half a Pound.

Put them in a Copper Pan, or a glazed Earthen one, upon a clear moderate Fire, stirring them continually with a wooden *Spatula* till the Mixture is become black, and almost of the Consistence of a Plaister, (which you may know by letting fall two or three Drops upon a Pewter Plate; for if they grow cold immediately, and do not stick to the Fingers, when touch'd, it is done enough.) Then must be added,

Of **Bees-Wax cut in little Bits**, an Ounce and a half.

Oil or Butter of Chocolate, an Ounce.

Balsam Capivi, an Ounce and a half.

When they are all melted and mixed together, the Pan must be taken off the Fire; and stirring constantly with the *Spatula*, you must add the following Ingredients, reduced into a fine Powder separately, and then well mixed together.

Lapis Calaminaris, heated in the Fire, and then quenched in Lime-Water, and ground upon a Porphyry, one Ounce.

Myrrh in Drops, } **Aloes Succotrine**, } of each two **Round Birth-wort**, } Drams. **Florentine Orris**, }

Camphire, a Dram.

When they are all well incorporated together, they must cool a little, and then be poured upon a Marble to be made into Rolls, after the ordinary Manner.

* * * * *

I have seen such surprizing Effects from this Emplaister, that I am almost backward to mention them, lest they should seem incredible. It cures the most stubborn and inveterate Ulcers, provided the Bone is not carious: for in this Case, lest you should lose your Labour, you must begin with the Bone, and then apply the Plaister. The Place must be dress'd Morning and Evening after it is clean'd with Lime Water, and wiped well with a Linnen Cloth.

The same Plaister may serve several Times, provided it be washed with Lime Water, wiped with a Rag, and held to the Fire a Moment before it is apply'd.

I exhort charitable People to make this Plaister and give it to the Poor, especially those that live in the Country; they will draw down a Thousand Blessings in this Life, and the Lord will recompence them hereafter.

An excellent Pomatum for Ringworms, Tettars, Pimples, and other Deformities of the Skin.

Take ***Flowers*** of ***Brimstone***[a], ***Salt Petre*** purified, of each Half an Ounce; good ***White Precipitate***[b], two Drams; ***Benzoin*** or ***Benjamin***, a Dram.

Beat the ***Benjamin*** and ***Salt-Petre*** a good while in a Brass Mortar, till they are reduced into a very fine Powder, then mix the Flower of Brimstone and White Precipitate with them and keep this Powder for Use.

* * * * *

At ***Martinico*** when I had occasion to make use of it, I incorporated it with Butter of Chocolate; but in ***France***, I substitute the best-scented ***Jessamin Pomatum***: This Smell, joined with that of Benjamin, corrects the Smell of the Brimstone, which some Persons abhor.

I cannot sufficiently recommend this ***Pomatum***, which always succeeds well, and I have often found it beneficial when every thing else fail'd.

You must not wonder if on the first, and sometimes the second Day, the Tettar seems more lively, or the Complection more dull; it is a sign that the Malignity is drawn out, and that the Seeds of it are destroy'd: you must therefore take heed of desisting, for the Skin in a little Time will be render'd as even and smooth as you can desire.

NOTES

[a] To wit, those that are made in **Holland**, if they can be got.

[b] To know if the **Precipitate** be good, you may do thus; Put a little upon a live Coal, if it flies away, it is good; if it stays behind, it is nothing but powder'd Ceruss, or some such thing.

FINIS.

www.bookjungle.com *email: sales@bookjungle.com fax: 630-214-0564 mail: Book Jungle PO Box 2226 Champaign, IL 61825*

The Codes Of Hammurabi And Moses
W. W. Davies

QTY

The discovery of the Hammurabi Code is one of the greatest achievements of archaeology, and is of paramount interest, not only to the student of the Bible, but also to all those interested in ancient history...

Religion   **ISBN:** *1-59462-338-4*   *Pages:132*
MSRP $12.95

The Theory of Moral Sentiments
Adam Smith

QTY

This work from 1749. contains original theories of conscience amd moral judgment and it is the foundation for systemof morals.

Philosophy   **ISBN:** *1-59462-777-0*   *Pages:536*
MSRP $19.95

Jessica's First Prayer
Hesba Stretton

QTY

In a screened and secluded corner of one of the many railway-bridges which span the streets of London there could be seen a few years ago, from five o'clock every morning until half past eight, a tidily set-out coffee-stall, consisting of a trestle and board, upon which stood two large tin cans, with a small fire of charcoal burning under each so as to keep the coffee boiling during the early hours of the morning when the work-people were thronging into the city on their way to their daily toil...

Childrens   **ISBN:** *1-59462-373-2*   *Pages:84*
MSRP $9.95

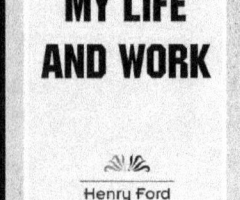

My Life and Work
Henry Ford

QTY

Henry Ford revolutionized the world with his implementation of mass production for the Model T automobile. Gain valuable business insight into his life and work with his own auto-biography... "We have only started on our development of our country we have not as yet, with all our talk of wonderful progress, done more than scratch the surface. The progress has been wonderful enough but..."

Biographies/   **ISBN:** *1-59462-198-5*   *Pages:300*
MSRP $21.95

www.bookjungle.com *email: sales@bookjungle.com fax: 630-214-0564 mail: Book Jungle PO Box 2226 Champaign, IL 61825*

The Art of Cross-Examination
Francis Wellman

I presume it is the experience of every author, after his first book is published upon an important subject, to be almost overwhelmed with a wealth of ideas and illustrations which could readily have been included in his book, and which to his own mind, at least, seem to make a second edition inevitable. Such certainly was the case with me; and when the first edition had reached its sixth impression in five months, I rejoiced to learn that it seemed to my publishers that the book had met with a sufficiently favorable reception to justify a second and considerably enlarged edition. ..

Reference ISBN: *1-59462-647-2* Pages:412 MSRP *$19.95*

On the Duty of Civil Disobedience
Henry David Thoreau

Thoreau wrote his famous essay, On the Duty of Civil Disobedience, as a protest against an unjust but popular war and the immoral but popular institution of slave-owning. He did more than write—he declined to pay his taxes, and was hauled off to gaol in consequence. Who can say how much this refusal of his hastened the end of the war and of slavery ?

Law ISBN: *1-59462-747-9* Pages:48 MSRP *$7.45*

Dream Psychology Psychoanalysis for Beginners
Sigmund Freud

Sigmund Freud, born Sigismund Schlomo Freud (May 6, 1856 - September 23, 1939), was a Jewish-Austrian neurologist and psychiatrist who co-founded the psychoanalytic school of psychology. Freud is best known for his theories of the unconscious mind, especially involving the mechanism of repression; his redefinition of sexual desire as mobile and directed towards a wide variety of objects; and his therapeutic techniques, especially his understanding of transference in the therapeutic relationship and the presumed value of dreams as sources of insight into unconscious desires.

Psychology ISBN: *1-59462-905-6* Pages:196 MSRP *$15.45*

The Miracle of Right Thought
Orison Swett Marden

Believe with all of your heart that you will do what you were made to do. When the mind has once formed the habit of holding cheerful, happy, prosperous pictures, it will not be easy to form the opposite habit. It does not matter how improbable or how far away this realization may see, or how dark the prospects may be, if we visualize them as best we can, as vividly as possible, hold tenaciously to them and vigorously struggle to attain them, they will gradually become actualized, realized in the life. But a desire, a longing without endeavor, a yearning abandoned or held indifferently will vanish without realization.

Self Help ISBN: *1-59462-644-8* Pages:360 MSRP *$25.45*

www.bookjungle.com email: sales@bookjungle.com fax: 630-214-0564 mail: Book Jungle PO Box 2226 Champaign, IL 61825

QTY

	Title	ISBN	Price
☐	**The Rosicrucian Cosmo-Conception Mystic Christianity** by *Max Heindel* *The Rosicrucian Cosmo-conception is not dogmatic, neither does it appeal to any other authority than the reason of the student. It is: not controversial, but is: sent forth in the, hope that it may help to clear...*	ISBN: *1-59462-188-8*	$38.95 New Age/Religion Pages 646
☐	**Abandonment To Divine Providence** by *Jean-Pierre de Caussade* *"The Rev. Jean Pierre de Caussade was one of the most remarkable spiritual writers of the Society of Jesus in France in the 18th Century. His death took place at Toulouse in 1751. His works have gone through many editions and have been republished..."*	ISBN: *1-59462-228-0*	$25.95 Inspirational/Religion Pages 400
☐	**Mental Chemistry** by *Charles Haanel* *Mental Chemistry allows the change of material conditions by combining and appropriately utilizing the power of the mind. Much like applied chemistry creates something new and unique out of careful combinations of chemicals the mastery of mental chemistry...*	ISBN: *1-59462-192-6*	$23.95 New Age Pages 354
☐	**The Letters of Robert Browning and Elizabeth Barret Barrett 1845-1846 vol II** by *Robert Browning and Elizabeth Barrett*	ISBN: *1-59462-193-4*	$35.95 Biographies Pages 596
☐	**Gleanings In Genesis (volume I)** by *Arthur W. Pink* *Appropriately has Genesis been termed "the seed plot of the Bible" for in it we have, in germ form, almost all of the great doctrines which are afterwards fully developed in the books of Scripture which follow...*	ISBN: *1-59462-130-6*	$27.45 Religion/Inspirational Pages 420
☐	**The Master Key** by *L. W. de Laurence* *In no branch of human knowledge has there been a more lively increase of the spirit of research during the past few years than in the study of Psychology, Concentration and Mental Discipline. The requests for authentic lessons in Thought Control, Mental Discipline and...*	ISBN: *1-59462-001-6*	$30.95 New Age/Business Pages 422
☐	**The Lesser Key Of Solomon Goetia** by *L. W. de Laurence* *This translation of the first book of the "Lemegton" which is now for the first time made accessible to students of Talismanic Magic was done, after careful collation and edition, from numerous Ancient Manuscripts in Hebrew, Latin, and French...*	ISBN: *1-59462-092-X*	$9.95 New Age/Occult Pages 92
☐	**Rubaiyat Of Omar Khayyam** by *Edward Fitzgerald* *Edward Fitzgerald, whom the world has already learned, in spite of his own efforts to remain within the shadow of anonymity, to look upon as one of the rarest poets of the century, was born at Bredfield, in Suffolk, on the 31st of March, 1809. He was the third son of John Purcell...*	ISBN: *1-59462-332-5*	$13.95 Music Pages 172
☐	**Ancient Law** by *Henry Maine* *The chief object of the following pages is to indicate some of the earliest ideas of mankind, as they are reflected in Ancient Law, and to point out the relation of those ideas to modern thought.*	ISBN: *1-59462-128-4*	$29.95 Religiom/History Pages 452
☐	**Far-Away Stories** by *William J. Locke* *"Good wine needs no bush, but a collection of mixed vintages does. And this book is just such a collection. Some of the stories I do not want to remain buried for ever in the museum files of dead magazine-numbers an author's not unpardonable vanity..."*	ISBN: *1-59462-129-2*	$19.45 Fiction Pages 272
☐	**Life of David Crockett** by *David Crockett* *"Colonel David Crockett was one of the most remarkable men of the times in which he lived. Born in humble life, but gifted with a strong will, an indomitable courage, and unremitting perseverance...*	ISBN: *1-59462-250-7*	$27.45 Biographies/New Age Pages 424
☐	**Lip-Reading** by *Edward Nitchie* *Edward B. Nitchie, founder of the New York School for the Hard of Hearing, now the Nitchie School of Lip-Reading, Inc, wrote "LIP-READING Principles and Practice". The development and perfecting of this meritorious work on lip-reading was an undertaking...*	ISBN: *1-59462-206-X*	$25.95 How-to Pages 400
☐	**A Handbook of Suggestive Therapeutics, Applied Hypnotism, Psychic Science** by *Henry Munro*	ISBN: *1-59462-214-0*	$24.95 Health/New Age/Health/Self-help Pages 376
☐	**A Doll's House: and Two Other Plays** by *Henrik Ibsen* *Henrik Ibsen created this classic when in revolutionary 1848 Rome. Introducing some striking concepts in playwriting for the realist genre, this play has been studied the world over.*	ISBN: *1-59462-112-8*	$19.95 Fiction/Classics/Plays 308
☐	**The Light of Asia** by *sir Edwin Arnold* *In this poetic masterpiece, Edwin Arnold describes the life and teachings of Buddha. The man who was to become known as Buddha to the world was born as Prince Gautama of India but he rejected the worldly riches and abandoned the reigns of power when...*	ISBN: *1-59462-204-3*	$13.95 Religion/History/Biographies Pages 170
☐	**The Complete Works of Guy de Maupassant** by *Guy de Maupassant* *"For days and days, nights and nights, I had dreamed of that first kiss which was to consecrate our engagement, and I knew not on what spot I should put my lips..."*	ISBN: *1-59462-157-8*	$16.95 Fiction/Classics Pages 240
☐	**The Art of Cross-Examination** by *Francis L. Wellman* *Written by a renowned trial lawyer, Wellman imparts his experience and uses case studies to explain how to use psychology to extract desired information through questioning.*	ISBN: *1-59462-309-0*	$26.95 How-to/Science/Reference Pages 408
☐	**Answered or Unanswered?** by *Louisa Vaughan* *Miracles of Faith in China*	ISBN: *1-59462-248-5*	$10.95 Religion Pages 112
☐	**The Edinburgh Lectures on Mental Science (1909)** by *Thomas* *This book contains the substance of a course of lectures recently given by the writer in the Queen Street Hall, Edinburgh. Its purpose is to indicate the Natural Principles governing the relation between Mental Action and Material Conditions...*	ISBN: *1-59462-008-3*	$11.95 New Age/Psychology Pages 148
☐	**Ayesha** by *H. Rider Haggard* *Verily and indeed it is the unexpected that happens! Probably if there was one person upon the earth from whom the Editor of this, and of a certain previous history, did not expect to hear again...*	ISBN: *1-59462-301-5*	$24.95 Classics Pages 380
☐	**Ayala's Angel** by *Anthony Trollope* *The two girls were both pretty, but Lucy who was twenty-one who supposed to be simple and comparatively unattractive, whereas Ayala was credited, as her Bombwhat romantic name might show, with poetic charm and a taste for romance. Ayala when her father died was nineteen...*	ISBN: *1-59462-352-X*	$29.95 Fiction Pages 484
☐	**The American Commonwealth** by *James Bryce* *An interpretation of American democratic political theory. It examines political mechanics and society from the perspective of Scotsman James Bryce*	ISBN: *1-59462-286-8*	$34.45 Politics Pages 572
☐	**Stories of the Pilgrims** by *Margaret P. Pumphrey* *This book explores pilgrims religious oppression in England as well as their escape to Holland and eventual crossing to America on the Mayflower, and their early days in New England...*	ISBN: *1-59462-116-0*	$17.95 History Pages 268

www.bookjungle.com email: sales@bookjungle.com fax: 630-214-0564 mail: Book Jungle PO Box 2226 Champaign, IL 61825

			QTY
The Fasting Cure by *Sinclair Upton*	ISBN: *1-59462-222-1*	**$13.95**	☐
In the Cosmopolitan Magazine for May, 1910, and in the Contemporary Review (London) for April, 1910, I published an article dealing with my experiences in fasting. I have written a great many magazine articles, but never one which attracted so much attention...	*New Age/Self Help/Health Pages 164*		
Hebrew Astrology by *Sepharial*	ISBN: *1-59462-308-2*	**$13.45**	☐
In these days of advanced thinking it is a matter of common observation that we have left many of the old landmarks behind and that we are now pressing forward to greater heights and to a wider horizon than that which represented the mind-content of our progenitors...	*Astrology Pages 144*		
Thought Vibration or The Law of Attraction in the Thought World	ISBN: *1-59462-127-6*	**$12.95**	☐
by *William Walker Atkinson*	*Psychology/Religion Pages 144*		
Optimism by *Helen Keller*	ISBN: *1-59462-108-X*	**$15.95**	☐
Helen Keller was blind, deaf, and mute since 19 months old, yet famously learned how to overcome these handicaps, communicate with the world, and spread her lectures promoting optimism. An inspiring read for everyone...	*Biographies/Inspirational Pages 84*		
Sara Crewe by *Frances Burnett*	ISBN: *1-59462-360-0*	**$9.45**	☐
In the first place, Miss Minchin lived in London. Her home was a large, dull, tall one, in a large, dull square, where all the houses were alike, and all the sparrows were alike, and where all the door-knockers made the same heavy sound...	*Childrens/Classic Pages 88*		
The Autobiography of Benjamin Franklin by *Benjamin Franklin*	ISBN: *1-59462-135-7*	**$24.95**	☐
The Autobiography of Benjamin Franklin has probably been more extensively read than any other American historical work, and no other book of its kind has had such ups and downs of fortune. Franklin lived for many years in England, where he was agent...	*Biographies/History Pages 332*		

Name	
Email	
Telephone	
Address	
City, State ZIP	

☐ Credit Card   ☐ Check / Money Order

Credit Card Number	
Expiration Date	
Signature	

Please Mail to: Book Jungle
                    PO Box 2226
                    Champaign, IL 61825
or Fax to: 630-214-0564

ORDERING INFORMATION

web: *www.bookjungle.com*
email: *sales@bookjungle.com*
fax: *630-214-0564*
mail: *Book Jungle PO Box 2226 Champaign, IL 61825*
or PayPal *to sales@bookjungle.com*

Please contact us for bulk discounts

DIRECT-ORDER TERMS

**20% Discount if You Order
Two or More Books**
Free Domestic Shipping!
Accepted: Master Card, Visa,
Discover, American Express

www.ingramcontent.com/pod-product-compliance
Lightning Source LLC
Chambersburg PA
CBHW081328040426
42453CB00013B/2342